# 101 BEST WEB SITES

# for SECONDARY
# TEACHERS

James Lerman

International Society for Technology in Education
EUGENE, OREGON • WASHINGTON, DC

# 101 BEST WEB SITES for SECONDARY TEACHERS
## James Lerman

**DIRECTOR OF PUBLISHING**
Jean Marie Hall

**ACQUISITIONS EDITOR**
Scott Harter

**PRODUCTION EDITOR**
Tracy Cozzens

**PRODUCTION COORDINATOR**
Amy Miller

**COPY EDITOR**
Nancy Olson

**BOOK DESIGN**
Kim McGovern, Tracy Cozzens

**COVER DESIGN**
Kim McGovern

**LAYOUT AND PRODUCTION**
Tracy Cozzens

**International Society for Technology in Education (ISTE)**
Washington, DC, Office:
    1710 Rhode Island Ave. NW, Suite 900, Washington, DC 20036-3132

Eugene, Oregon, Office:
    175 West Broadway, Suite 300, Eugene, OR 97401–3003
Order Desk: 1.800.336.5191
Order Fax: 1.541.302.3778
Customer Service: orders@iste.org
Book Publishing: books@iste.org
Rights and Permissions: permissions@iste.org
Web: www.iste.org

**First Edition**
ISBN 978-1-56484-216-9

# ABOUT ISTE

The International Society for Technology in Education (ISTE) is a nonprofit professional organization with a worldwide membership of leaders in education technology. We are dedicated to promoting appropriate uses of technology to support and improve learning, teaching, and administration in PK–12 and teacher education. As part of that mission, ISTE provides high-quality and timely information, services, and materials, such as this book.

ISTE Book Publishing works with experienced educators to develop and produce practical resources for classroom teachers, teacher educators, and technology leaders. Every manuscript we select for publication is carefully peer-reviewed and professionally edited. We look for content that emphasizes the effective use of technology where it can make a difference—increasing the productivity of teachers and administrators; helping students with unique learning styles, abilities, or backgrounds; collecting and using data for decision making at the school and district levels; and creating dynamic, project-based learning environments that engage 21st-century learners. We value your feedback on this book and other ISTE products. E-mail us at **books@iste.org**.

ISTE is home of the National Educational Technology Standards (NETS) Project, the National Educational Computing Conference (NECC), and the National Center for Preparing Tomorrow's Teachers to Use Technology (NCPT3). To find out more about these and other ISTE initiatives and to view our complete book list or request a print catalog, visit our Web site at **www.iste.org**. You'll find information about:

- ISTE, our mission, and our members
- Membership opportunities and services
- Online communities and special interest groups (SIGs)
- Professional development services
- Research and evaluation services
- Educator resources
- ISTE's National Educational Technology Standards (NETS) for Students, Teachers, and Administrators
- *Learning & Leading with Technology* magazine
- *Journal of Research on Technology in Education*

# ABOUT THE AUTHOR

**James Lerman** designs educational environments and experiences for learners of all ages, from preschool through graduate school and beyond. Design is a particular passion of his, as are technology, politics, and the arts. He has been a classroom teacher, principal, staff development director, director of technology, assistant superintendent of schools, college professor, nonprofit organization executive, national conference presenter, consultant, founder of four public schools, and author. *101 Best Web Sites for Secondary Teachers* is Mr. Lerman's second ISTE book. His first book, *101 Best Web Sites for Elementary Teachers*, was published earlier this year.

## Dedication

To my great-grandmother, Bobka Lerman, who came to America at the turn of the last century from Russia (Ukraine), with no one and nothing except her two very young sons and her extraordinary bravery, determination, and strength.

## Acknowledgments

I am very grateful to the folks at ISTE for giving me the opportunity to write this book. Scott Harter, Jean Marie Hall, Amy Miller, and Tracy Cozzens have been patient, helpful, thoughtful, and supportive. I also want to deeply thank my wife, Terry, and my daughter, Michela, for putting up with the large and small inconveniences created by the time and energy I devoted to this project.

# Contents

## CHAPTER 4 • General Teacher Support — 51

## CHAPTER 5 • Health and PE — 65

# Introduction

I f you're a teacher, you know that most people have no idea how challenging, complex, and time-consuming your job is. You've probably heard the refrain a thousand times: "Oh, teaching is a great job. You work half a day and have the whole summer off."

Words to that effect are a sure sign the speaker fails to appreciate how much out-of-class preparation, in-class pressure, and after-class follow-up are required for teachers to do a high-quality, professional job.

You know better, of course; educators are constantly busy, and to do their jobs well, they have a tremendous need for ready and reliable information. Internet resources can be exceptionally valuable, yet teachers often lack the time to locate and discover the best the World Wide Web has to offer. There may be buried treasure out there in the wilderness, but most teachers can't afford to go digging around for it at random. If only there were a road map . . . .

Searchers, educators, your map is here, in this book!

That vast, confounding World Wide Web territory has been thoroughly searched; this guide-book is the result. Specifically, *101 Best Web Sites for Secondary Teachers* assembles in one place an outstanding compilation of Internet resources devoted to making your work easier, more efficient, and more productive.

The selected Web sites have been organized into 10 chapters, covering all the major subject areas of the secondary curriculum as well as a few special sections devoted to "College and Career Planning," "General Teacher Support," and "Technology Integration."

Each chapter begins with a brief discussion of the chapter's highlights. This is followed by a Quick Reference Chart, which indicates the principal features of each site—both for teachers and students. Sites are organized alphabetically, with the name and Internet address (URL), a screenshot, and a written summary that includes a site description and highlights for teachers.

*Please note:* Within each summary, all **active links** appear in bold text. For ease of entering the listed URLs in your browser, we do not include the http:// prefix. All up-to-date Web browsers will automatically add this after you type in the domain name.

The book concludes with a chart that correlates each of the selected Web sites with the National Educational Technology Standards for both students and teachers, as developed by ISTE.

# HOW THE SITES WERE CHOSEN

Many, many sources were consulted in compiling this book. They included professional magazines and journals, online newsletters, books, conference presentations, recommendations by colleagues, lists of outstanding sites by individuals and organizations, and the results of numerous queries, which were tracked down using a variety of search engines.

To be selected as one of the *101 Best Web Sites for Secondary Teachers*, a Web site had to demonstrate

- ease of access,
- ease of navigation,
- valuable and relevant content,
- credible and reliable content,
- free availability.

When more than one Web site addressed the same topic, the site or sites that were best at what they did (in the author's opinion) were chosen. Sites that charge for their services have not been included unless free resources are offered along with services or information that carry a cost. However, many of the growing number of valuable Web sites that charge a subscription fee are worth their modest cost and should be considered if no comparable free site is offered on the same topic.

Of course, these 101 sites are but a fraction of the hundreds of thousands of sites created by and for educators, many of which are excellent and deserve mention. While it may be clear why very extensive sites such as MarcoPolo or AOL@SCHOOL were selected, the rationale for choosing those that are more narrowly focused, such as John F. Barber, Ph.D.; Arts for Academic Achievement; or Nicenet Internet Classroom Assistant, may not be so obvious. Another author might have made different selections.

I felt it was important to include a variety of Web sites in this collection and have selected sites created by professional organizations, universities, and recipients of government or foundation grants, as well as sites created by individuals who are simply trying to provide a useful service to their colleagues. Some of the ones chosen consist primarily of long lists of links to other sites; if so, they do that job exceptionally well. Other sites provide original content for both students *and* teachers. Still others may direct themselves solely to students *or* teachers. Some sites include lesson plans, others don't. Some have free e-mail newsletters, some don't. Some attempt to cover broad topics in great depth, others try to do one simple thing and do it well.

Sites that used the communicative power of the Internet in unique or powerful ways had special appeal. Sites with interactive or multimedia material for teachers and students were particularly attractive.

# FINDING A MISSING SITE

If you've used the Internet for any length of time, you know that sites may appear or disappear without warning. They may change their names, move to another location, become part of another site, or simply vanish. It can be quite frustrating.

All the sites listed in this book were checked just before its publication. At that time, names and URLs were accurate. If, however, you attempt to reach a site and aren't successful, I can offer a number of suggestions:

1. Check very carefully that you have entered the site's address accurately. A single erroneous keystroke, an extra space or period, a capitalized letter that should be lowercase—all will take you down a dead-end road. If at first you don't succeed, check carefully and try again.

2. Wait a few moments and try the site again. It's possible to experience the Internet equivalent of a "busy signal" when trying to connect to a popular Web site. Sometimes, if you just try again later, it will work fine.

3. Using any search engine, enter the name (not the URL) of the Web site you're seeking, then scroll through the results to locate the site. Like many people these days, I use Google (**www.google.com**) for most of my Web searching and recommend it highly.

4. Trim the URL by eliminating elements of the address starting at the right. This can be especially effective with very long Web addresses. You trim a URL by eliminating, one step at a time, everything in between slashes (/). For example, consider the fictional URL **http://www.jameslerman.com/private/public/101bestwebsites/tools/index.htm**. To trim it, you would first delete **index.htm** and try to access the now shortened address. Then eliminate **tools/** and try again. Then eliminate **101bestwebsites/** and try again. Eventually you'll reach a Web page that opens. Once you arrive there, look for hyperlinks (usually underlined words in blue) or titles that resemble what you're seeking.

5. When all else fails, you can try the archive at the Wayback Machine. This unique and marvelous Web site attempts to store a copy of every site on the Web. With something like 5 billion available Web sites as of July 2004, it's a very big job. Fortunately, most of the sites educators are likely to be looking for will be sufficiently large or prominent to merit the Wayback Machine's attention. The URL is **webdev.archive.org**.

   Once you arrive at Wayback, enter into the search box the URL of the site you're trying to reach. If it's in the archive, Wayback will give you hyperlinks to the site you're seeking, one for each time it was archived. The process is a little complicated, but I've used Wayback many times, with about a 75% success rate.

# MAKING USE OF PLUG-INS

Plug-ins are free software programs that enable users to play audio or video and display PDF files (among other things). This book assumes the computer you use to access the Internet has any needed plug-ins already loaded. The process is free and quite simple. If you don't know how to do it, ask a colleague or one of your students to explain. If you're using a school or district computer, you may need to contact your network administrator to download and activate the plug-ins.

Plug-ins used by many of the best Web sites include:

**Adobe Reader:** www.adobe.com/products/acrobat/readermain.html (Under Downloads in the left-hand menu, click on **Free Adobe Reader**. This program allows you to read and print files that are in PDF format.)

**Macromedia Flash Player:** www.macromedia.com (Click on **Download Flash Player**.)

**Java Plug-in:** java.sun.com/products/plugin/

**QuickTime Player:** www.apple.com/quicktime/ (Click on the link for the free version of the player.)

**RealPlayer:** www.real.com (Look for the small print that directs you to the free version of RealPlayer.)

**Shockwave Player:** www.macromedia.com (Click on **Download Shockwave Player**.)

To repeat, all these plug-ins are free. It's possible to purchase enhanced versions for some, which provide superior performance, but it is absolutely not necessary. The plug-ins are available for both PCs and Macs and will not compromise your computer's performance.

This book also assumes you are accessing the Internet over a connection that is faster than a 56K modem. Users need to access the Web on a high-speed connection if they are to readily view videos or listen to audio files. High-speed connections come in a variety of formats, including DSL, cable, T1, or T3. Thanks to the E-rate program, most schools have the necessary Internet connections.

## USING AN ONLINE BOOKMARK SERVICE

I highly recommend using an online bookmark service, if you don't already. Three service sites are listed below. What they enable you to do is store your favorite bookmarks online, rather than on your computer. They're all free. Two of them store URLs only. The third, Furl, can store whole Web sites as well as the URLs. If you store a Web site on Furl, you don't have to worry that it will suddenly disappear from the Internet; it's always there on Furl's server, fully searchable and saved to your account.

Using an online bookmark (or "favorites") service has a number of advantages.

1. If you use more than one computer (one at school and one at home, for example), you don't have to worry about which computer has the bookmark you need. You can access all your bookmarks from any computer that has Internet access.

2. When you buy a new computer, or lose or break your laptop, you don't have to transfer or re-enter your bookmarks.

3. You may make your bookmarks public or private, or both. If you want your students to access certain Web sites for a particular unit or project, you can create a unique space for that one activity only and enter all the Web sites there for students to access at school, home, or another remote location. This eliminates the tedious process of correcting typing errors when entering long URLs.

   In the same way, you can also share useful Web sites with colleagues. You can place the URLs in a folder and e-mail the whole folder. You may keep your bookmarks private, available only to you, or you may protect them so that they're available only to people who have the password you create.

4. You can easily set up multiple folders and move, delete, or rename URLs.

5. You can add notes to help you remember what's special or unique about any particular Web site.

6. You can set up a shortcut that enables you to add any Web site to your list with just a few easy keystrokes.

7. If you use multiple Web browsers (such as Explorer and Netscape), all your bookmarks can be saved in one location, on one list.

The Web-based bookmarking services are:

**Backflip:** www.backflip.com

**Furl:** www.furl.net

**iKeepBookmarks:** www.ikeepbookmarks.com

# INTERNET SECURITY BASICS

While the Internet offers a wide array of useful resources, accessing them can also make your computer vulnerable to a host of problems. In the old days, viruses were spread primarily through infected floppies or e-mail attachments, but now they can gain access to your system in a variety of ways, including the Internet.

Malicious programs can lurk anywhere online—in an interactive Web application, a Java applet, or a poisoned cookie. Automated programs roam the Internet looking for vulnerable systems to attack and personal information to steal. Once the damage to your system is done, it's difficult to set things right; sometimes even a computer technician can't save your infected files or corrupted data.

While the information technology (IT) team at your school or district works to protect your network's security, team members rely on the support of users who practice "safe surfing." At work, being aware of security threats helps maintain the integrity of your system and the confidentiality of your data. At home, you're likely on your own, so awareness is even more essential.

Threats can be broken down into three major categories, each with its own particular set of countermeasures:

## Malware

Malware is malicious software designed to damage computer files or disrupt system and network operations. Here are definitions of the most common types.

**VIRUS.** Just like its disease-causing counterpart in nature, a virus is a piece of computer code that is able to replicate itself once it's found a host (your computer). A virus can be downloaded without your knowledge and execute or run itself without your permission. Because it copies itself over and over, even the simplest virus can cause problems. Viruses can quickly use up a computer's available memory, making the system inoperable. Viruses can also carry a "payload"—malicious code that corrupts and destroys crucial files on your computer. While Windows computers continue to be the predominant target of virus writers, Unix/Linux and Macintosh computers aren't immune.

**WORM.** A worm, like a virus, can replicate rapidly, bringing a computer system to a standstill by using up available memory. Unlike a virus, a worm doesn't hide in, or attach itself to, another file or program; it's a stand-alone program that roams networks autonomously, bogging down computers, destroying files, stealing passwords and credit card numbers, and opening back doors.

**TROJAN HORSE.** Named after the gift horse of Trojan War fame, this malware masquerades as a free game or useful utility program. Once it's downloaded onto your computer, it can unleash a worm or keylogger, or open a back door into your system.

**BACK DOOR.** A program that runs secretly on a computer, opening a hole in its security that allows outsiders access to the system. A back door typically opens a connection to the Internet and broadcasts a message detectable by "port scanners" that hackers use to find vulnerable computers. Once the hacker accesses your system through the back door, he can steal personal information, corrupt data, or commandeer your computer and use it with other compromised computers to create a "zombie network." Zombie networks have been used to launch denial-of-service attacks on Web sites and flood e-mail servers with virus-laden or spoofed e-mails.

**KEYLOGGER.** This is another program that runs secretly on a computer, tracking every keystroke a user makes and sending that information back to the program's creator. Keyloggers are most often used to steal credit card numbers, passwords, or other personal information.

How can you protect yourself from these virtual contagions? While there's no surefire way to immunize your system from every possible attack, here are steps you can take to make infection from malware much less likely.

1. **Purchase antivirus software.** Numerous high-quality antivirus programs are available to protect against viruses, worms, and Trojan horses. Some of them are even free. Norton

Antivirus and McAfee VirusScan are the two most popular choices, but other good choices include PC-Cillin Internet Security, Panda Antivirus, BitDefender, and AVG Antivirus. While many free antivirus programs are advertised on the Internet, be wary: in the past, several infamous Trojan horses have masqueraded as free antivirus programs. Talk with your IT team to learn what programs they recommend.

2. **Regularly update your antivirus software.** This can't be emphasized too strongly. An out-of-date antivirus program is just as dangerous as no antivirus protection. With new viruses and variants of old viruses released every day, it's imperative that your program's virus definitions be updated as often as possible. Most good antivirus programs automate this process. When you purchase the software, you also purchase a subscription to virus definition updates. The program will automatically search for new definitions every time you connect to the Internet (or every few hours if your computer is always connected). If new definitions are found, they are downloaded and added to your program's "hit list" of malicious code to watch out for. This subscription is limited to a specific length of time, usually a year. To continue to receive updates, you need to renew your subscription.

3. **Use your antivirus software.** This may seem obvious, but many people aren't using their antivirus program effectively. Be sure your program is configured to automatically scan any file before it's opened or executed. This is typically the default setting for the program. You should also schedule regular full-system scans—scans of every file on your hard drive—to check for malware that may have snuck in unannounced.

4. **Be careful with e-mail.** Special care should be taken with e-mail and e-mail attachments, still the most common vehicle for malware transmission. Good antivirus programs will automatically scan e-mails before downloading them, since viruses can hide in an image or script embedded in the message itself (not just in an attachment). Make sure this feature is turned on.

5. **Be careful with Internet downloads.** Take special care with any program you download from the Internet. Legitimate software programs are "signed." This means the distributor has verified the safety of the download and can be held responsible for any problems. Unsigned downloads may be malware, so don't accept them! Ask your IT team how to configure your Internet browser so that it won't accept any unsigned downloads. When you do download a program, carefully read the software use policy or agreement before installing it. Free programs such as screensavers, media plug-ins, and file-sharing utilities are frequently bundled with programs that may be adware or spyware, so be sure you aren't agreeing to install any programs you don't want.

## Spyware

Spyware is software that gathers data about you and the way you use your computer, usually for commercial purposes. It has quickly come to rival viruses and spam e-mails as a major problem for Internet users.

Spyware comes in many forms, invading your computer without your knowledge or consent. It can arrive attached to programs you've downloaded. It can also come in the form of "tracking cookies" uploaded to your computer when you visit a particular Web site. Once on your computer, the spyware compromises your privacy by gathering data (such as what Web sites you visit or what you buy online) and, through your Internet connection, transmitting the data back to the Web site's originator. You may not be aware at first that spyware is running on your computer. However, as it accumulates on your hard drive, your system will start to bog down.

Like any other program, spyware runs by using your computer's memory. It also uses up some of your Internet bandwidth to communicate with its maker. If you have these programs running in the background, your computer may lack the system resources to run programs you *want* to run, and your Internet connection will slow to a crawl. Poorly written spyware can even crash your system.

While most spyware targets users with advertisements for specific products and services (an alternative name is adware), some varieties truly earn malware status. The most common are browser hijackers—spyware programs that change your Internet browser settings. Browser hijackers change your home page without your consent and typically add links to other sites (often pornographic in nature) to your list of Bookmarks or Favorites. This is not just a nuisance issue: a few cases have been reported of employees losing their jobs because of Web links found on their computer that may have been placed there by hijackers. Sometimes a hijack program will deny you access to antivirus and anti-spyware Web sites, or even disable the antivirus software on your computer.

Browser hijackers get onto your computer just like other spyware programs. They can be bundled together with free utility programs and games, so be sure to read the software use policy carefully before installing anything you download from the Internet. Another popular technique is the pop-up download, in which a small window pops up on your screen when you visit a particular site, informing you that you need to download a program to "optimize" your browser or view all of the content on that site. These messages are deceptively worded to encourage you to select "Yes" and agree to the download; they often look and sound like the update reminders from legitimate programs already on your computer, so read carefully!

Finally, and most alarmingly, there is the "drive-by download," in which the hijacker is downloaded invisibly when you visit a site or read an HTML e-mail message. The first clue that your browser has been hijacked may come when you notice your home page has suddenly changed, or when you find yourself being redirected to questionable sites whenever you try to navigate away from the page you're viewing.

Among the growing number of anti-spyware programs available for purchase or free download, the most popular are Ad-aware and Spybot Search and Destroy (other titles include SpywareBlaster and SpywareGuide's X-Blaster). Also, antivirus programs now often provide spyware protection. Because of the numerous forms spyware can take, it's a good idea to have more than one anti-spyware solution.

Remember that downloading and installing anti-spyware software isn't enough: you need to update the spyware definitions daily or weekly (just as you do with your antivirus program) and scan your system regularly. It's also crucial that you download and install any security patches and updates available for your system.

## Spoofing

Spoofing is a technique used by hackers to gain unauthorized access to a computer or network share. Spoofing involves the crafting of an e-mail message or Web site that appears to be coming from a trusted source—a computer or software manufacturer, a bank or credit card company, your Internet service provider, and so forth. Spoofed messages will often direct the user to download a patch or update (launching a back door or keylogger instead), or visit an official-looking Web site where the same kind of malware awaits. Sometimes, the message will ask for passwords and other personal information that can be used to gain direct access to the user's computer or network accounts.

Spoofing works because the author of the message or Web site has stolen the IP address (the number that uniquely identifies a computer connected to the Internet) of the trusted source and has altered the packets of information coming from the author's own machine so that it appears they are coming from that source. In other words, the message or site appears to be coming from a Microsoft or Citibank server rather than Hank Hacker's computer. Spoofed e-mails can be subtly persuasive or officious and intimidating and are difficult for less experienced users to resist. Recently, spoofed messages have been created that require no action at all from the user; instead, a script embedded in the message itself launches the malicious program once the user views it.

Whether or not they're spoofing, hackers find a way to exploit vulnerabilities in new software almost immediately, then they post their discoveries on Web sites for others to enjoy and use. These security holes then become the targets of viruses, worms, and malware of every description. The Windows operating system and such Microsoft programs as Internet Explorer and Outlook Express have been notoriously vulnerable to such attacks. Hackers have targeted Windows primarily because it's the predominant operating system throughout the world, not because the Macintosh OS or Unix/Linux is invulnerable to attack.

## How to protect yourself

Start by making sure you always download and install all critical security updates for your operating system and software. This update process has been automated for Windows and Macintosh computers. So as long as you have your computer configured to automatically accept all critical updates (the default setting), you'll be closing any security holes as soon as patches are available. One caveat: because some security updates have caused problems for network administrators, your IT team may want to research compatibility issues before you install updates.

Firewalls prevent unauthorized access to your system by filtering every packet of information coming in from or going out to the Internet, then blocking traffic that doesn't meet its security criteria. Firewalls can be built into hardware (such as network routers and gateways) or software (programs from Norton, McAfee, ZoneAlarm, Sygate, and many others). Your school or district is almost certainly using firewalls to protect the network from attack. If you also have a personal firewall installed on your work computer, check with IT personnel to make sure it's properly configured and isn't interfering with network security or your ability to use the Web.

### If you find yourself in trouble

Keeping up-to-date on all the potential vulnerabilities of computers and networks is a full-time job for security experts and not something you should expect to handle yourself. If you suspect that your computer has fallen prey to any of the attacks described in this section, contact your IT team immediately and describe the problem to the experts. If your system has been compromised by a hacker, it's quite likely that other computers on your network have also been compromised. Resolving security intrusions and repairing the damage they can cause are jobs for trained network technicians.

Your IT team is your first stop if your school or office computer becomes infected. If you experience a problem on your home computer, several nonprofit Web sites offer free advice and information to help you get out of sticky situations, such as a hijacked browser home page or a virus infection. Sometimes entering a description of the problem in a search engine will direct you to a solution. One helpful site is Tech Support Guy (**www.techguy.org**). This site is run by knowledgeable volunteers and is supported by donations, usually from grateful Internet surfers who have been helped out of jams. Once you've registered, you can post your problem to a forum. Registration is free.

# PROVIDING FEEDBACK

I sincerely hope educators will find this volume to be useful and informative. If you have any feedback, please feel free to contact me at **jwriter@earthlink.net**. I'm particularly interested in hearing about your experiences with the listed Web sites and learning whether you have others to suggest for consideration. This will be helpful to me in my work as a conference presenter, a technology trainer, and the author of the second edition of *101 Best Web Sites for Secondary Teachers*.

JAMES LERMAN

# CHAPTER 1

# The Arts

The seven Web sites listed in this chapter are host to hundreds of lesson plans and interdisciplinary projects for teaching fine arts. The Museum of Modern Art (MoMA), the National Gallery of Art, and For Teachers have wonderful collections of art as well as multimedia virtual exhibits and tours. TeachingArts.org provides numerous resources for assessment in the arts, technology in the arts, and arts for English language learners and special populations. Arts for Academic Achievement documents how arts programs can improve students' overall academic achievement. On the Jazz site, visitors can listen to samples from many famous jazz recordings, and they can play a virtual piano that allows them to experiment with various styles of jazz. Make sure you check out the free teaching resources available from the National Gallery of Art, and remember to check out ARTSEDGE, sponsored by the Kennedy Center in Washington, D.C. (described under the MarcoPolo site in chapter 4, "General Teacher Support").

The Web sites in this chapter offer extensive background information on the arts, arts history, and arts interpretation—often in compelling multimedia formats. A great variety of interactive experiences awaits the adventurous!

# QUICK REFERENCE CHART

| The Arts | FEATURES FOR TEACHERS | | | | | | |
|---|---|---|---|---|---|---|---|
| Name of Site/URL | chat or forum | lesson plans | teacher resources | parent resources | teacher's guide | video, audio, applets | Web links |
| **ArtsConnectEd**<br>www.artsconnected.org | | ■ | ■ | ■ | ■ | | ■ |
| **Arts for Academic Achievement: The Annenberg Challenge**<br>education.umn.edu/CAREI/Reports/Annenberg/ | | | | *Research Reports* | | | |
| **For Teachers (Getty Education)**<br>www.getty.edu/education/for_teachers | ■ | ■ | ■ | ■ | ■ | | ■ |
| **Jazz**<br>www.pbs.org/jazz | ■ | ■ | ■ | | ■ | ■ | ■ |
| **MoMA Educational Resources**<br>www.moma.org/education/multimedia.html | ■ | ■ | ■ | ■ | ■ | | ■ |
| **National Gallery of Art: Education**<br>www.nga.gov/education/education.htm | ■ | ■ | ■ | ■ | ■ | | ■ |
| **TeachingArts.org**<br>www.teachingarts.org | | ■ | ■ | ■ | ■ | ■ | ■ |

The shaded boxes indicate the feature is available on the Web site.

# QUICK REFERENCE CHART *(continued)*

| The Arts | FEATURES FOR TEACHERS | | | FEATURES FOR STUDENTS | | |
|---|---|---|---|---|---|---|
| **Name of Site/URL** | assessment ideas | e-newsletter | reproducibles | activities | interactive exercises | reading material |
| **ArtsConnectEd** www.artsconnected.org | | | | | | |
| **Arts for Academic Achievement: The Annenberg Challenge** education.umn.edu/CAREI/Reports/ Annenberg/ | | *Research Reports* | | | | |
| **For Teachers (Getty Education)** www.getty.edu/education/for_teachers | | | | | | |
| **Jazz** www.pbs.org/jazz | | | | | | |
| **MoMA Educational Resources** www.moma.org/education/ multimedia.html | | *Education E-News* | | | | |
| **National Gallery of Art: Education** www.nga.gov/education/education.htm | | | | | | |
| **TeachingArts.org** www.teachingarts.org | | | | | | |

The shaded boxes indicate the feature is available on the Web site.

## ArtsConnectEd

**www.artsconnected.org**

**SITE DESCRIPTION:** The designers of this Web site refer to it with the abbreviation ACE, and ace it is. Developed jointly by the Minneapolis Institute of Arts and the Walker Art Center, it aims "to make arts education timely, engaging, interactive, and pertinent for both teachers and students of all ages." ACE is divided into five main sections: **Art Gallery**, **For Your Classroom**, **Library & Archives**, **Playground**, and **Search**. At any point in your visit, you may select a work of art and add it to your personal online collection. You may then save it, print it, or e-mail it to someone. **Art Gallery** also contains more than 20 tours and adventures, which are self-contained interactive experiences focusing on such themes and topics as Native American art, the Prairie School of Architecture (including Frank Lloyd Wright), photography, and much more. Many of these contain a teacher's guide for use with students at various grade levels.

**HIGHLIGHTS FOR TEACHERS:** The most teacher-friendly area of ACE is **For Your Classroom**. The main page for this area allows visitors to download the complete 28-page Teacher's Guide to the whole ACE site and also gives access to **ArtsNetMinnesota** (ANM). ANM organizes works of art by theme and then guides students through activities and reflections designed to develop a deeper understanding of art. The themes are **Environment**, **Inner Worlds**, **Identity**, **What Is Art?**, and **Designing Spaces and Places**. Of particular note is the **Search Wizard** located on the **For Your Classroom** page. It enables you to easily and quickly select ACE resources by grade level. Many of ACE's interactive exercises are unique and outstanding. For example, the **Artist's Toolkit** (accessible through **Art Gallery**) enables users to explore visual elements and principles by watching an animated demonstration, finding examples in works of art, and creating their own artwork online. The site links to Wigs, another activity in which users may manipulate elements: viewers are presented with the face of a model and, by adding different colors and styles of wigs, they can explore issues of identity and image (**www.walkerart.org/ education/activities/simpson/interactive.html**).

## Arts for Academic Achievement: The Annenberg Challenge

education.umn.edu/CAREI/Reports/Annenberg/

**SITE DESCRIPTION:** The arts are consistently overlooked in our constant search for ways to improve student achievement. This is the only Web site in the book devoted strictly to research, and it gathers solid evidence that arts education plays an important role in improving overall student achievement. It articulates that position persuasively. This research is so powerful and important, it deserves to be seen by the widest possible audience.

The Arts for Academic Achievement (AAA) program was funded by the Annenberg Foundation. The Center for Applied Research and Educational Improvement (**CAREI**) at the University of Minnesota was the third-party documenter and evaluator for a three-year program conducted in the Minneapolis public schools. Although primarily carried out in elementary schools, participation included three middle schools and seven high schools. Similar research outcomes for secondary school students are reported elsewhere by noted Stanford University professor Shirley Brice Heath (**www.shirleybriceheath.com**).

**HIGHLIGHTS FOR TEACHERS:** The following quotes are from the *Summative Evaluation Report,* written by Debra Ingram and Karen R. Seashore and published in October 2003:

> "Our analyses indicate a significant relationship between arts integrated instruction and improved student learning in reading and mathematics in the AAA program . . . . AAA assisted all types of students, not just those who were already doing well in school." (p. 3) "The major change[s in student-student interaction] we observed included the following:
>
> - Improved communication in groups.
>
> - The emergence of unlikely leaders.
>
> - The blending of special needs children into their peer group.
>
> - Improved student teamwork to accomplish a goal . . . " (pp. 5–6).
>
> "AAA . . . brought about substantial change in teachers' instructional practice and their role in improving schools, both pre-requisites to any lasting change in student achievement . . . . Instruction became more child-focused, teachers expanded their toolkit of instructional strategies, [and they] changed perceptions about student capacity." (pp. 6–7).

## For Teachers (Getty Education)

**www.getty.edu/education/for_teachers**

**SITE DESCRIPTION:** This is the home page for K–12 teachers at the J. Paul Getty Museum in Los Angeles. The Getty has long been involved in promoting fine arts education, and this site supports that purpose very well. It offers six exceptionally well-organized and well-designed collections of lessons, as well as the separate **ArtsEdNet** site. The art focuses primarily (but not exclusively) on the European and American traditions.

The lesson collections (both K–12 and adult) are titled: **Looking at Decorative Arts**, **Looking at Portraits**, **Language Through Art: An ESL Enrichment Curriculum** (adult), **About Life: The Photographs of Dorothea Lange**, **Art & Language Arts: Ideas for the Classroom**, and **Devices of Wonder: Teaching Tools**.

**HIGHLIGHTS FOR TEACHERS:** ArtsEdNet is divided into four main areas: **Lesson Plans & Curriculum Ideas**, **Image Galleries & Exhibitions**, **ArtsEdNet Talk**, and **Search & Index**. The lesson plans may be accessed either by grade level or alphabetically. They range from single class periods to full units. The **Getty Scope & Sequence** link leads to a full K–12 guide for teaching art. The artwork in ArtsEdNet displays a considerably more diverse approach than the museum as a whole.

Art may be located by artist, title, or date. You'll find seven professional artists' galleries and two student galleries. Links are provided to Getty exhibitions of the Roman Forum, the art of Ancient Greece and Rome, and **Making Architecture**, an exhibit of the renowned Getty Center itself.

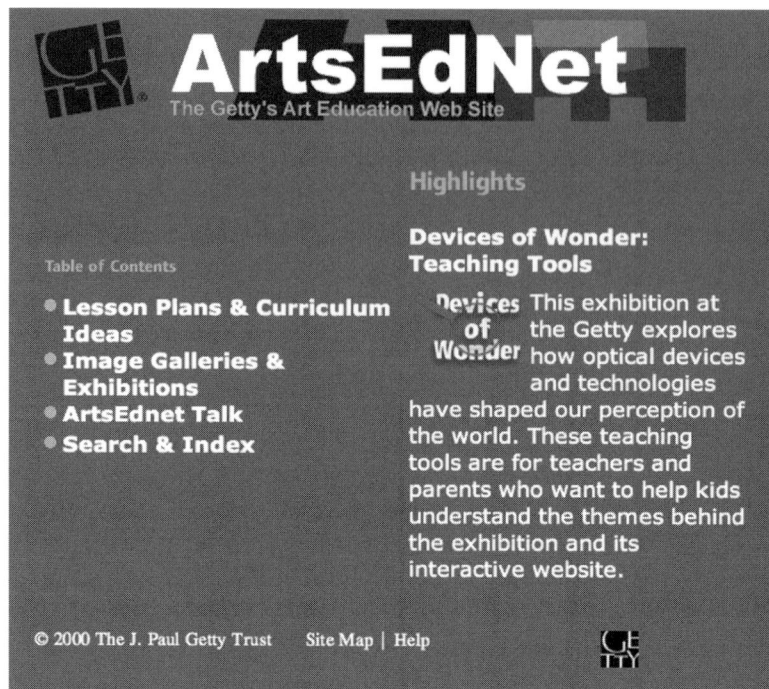

## Jazz

**www.pbs.org/jazz**

**SITE DESCRIPTION:** This is the Web site created to accompany the famed 10-part Ken Burns documentary series *Jazz,* originally broadcast on PBS in 2001. Just as the film series attempted to capture the breadth and depth of "America's classical music" in about 20 hours of video, this Web site tries to do the same, albeit in a different medium. Both efforts succeed to a remarkable degree.

Jazz (the Web site) is divided into 13 separate sections. Some of the highlights include: **Places, Spaces & Changing Faces**, which uncovers the roots of jazz by examining the major venues of the four cities where jazz originated; **Jazz Lounge**, where visitors can learn about the structures and styles of jazz; **Musical Notes**, which lists famous recordings and selected discographies; and **Biographies**, where visitors can learn about more than 100 major figures in jazz history. Several other sections offer essays on the interplay between jazz and American history.

**HIGHLIGHTS FOR TEACHERS:** From an audio sample of Louis Armstrong playing 1931's "Stardust" to Thelonius Monk playing "Round Midnight" in 1968, from a virtual piano that enables visitors to watch as well as play in a variety of musical styles to profiles and biographies of famous places and people, this site is full of resources to help young people develop an understanding and appreciation for jazz.

The **Classroom** area gives visitors access to numerous well-constructed lessons and activities for students in Grades K–5 and 6–12. Also located here is the excellent **General Motors Music Study Guide for Grades 5–8**. On the last page is a wonderful listening guide sheet for students.

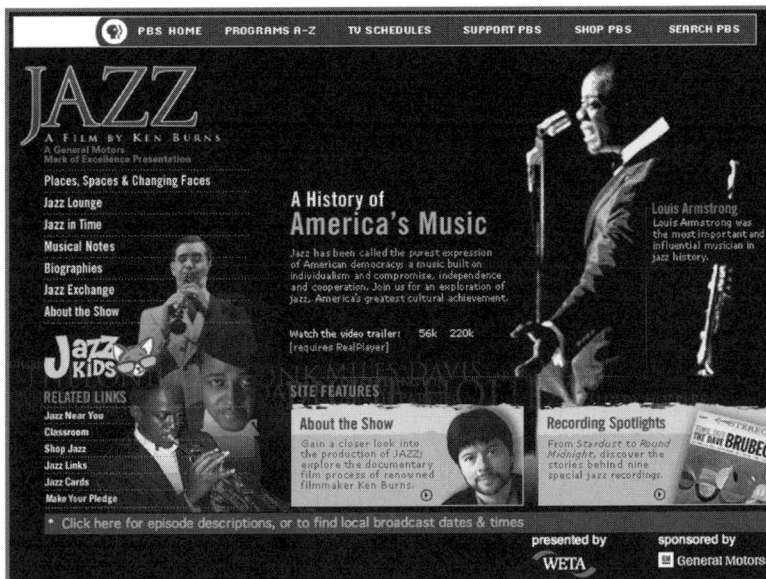

## MoMA Educational Resources

www.moma.org/education/multimedia.html

**SITE DESCRIPTION:** This unassuming page serves as the portal to the Education Department of the Museum of Modern Art (MoMA) in New York City. While the page may be plain, the resources most definitely are not.

Visitors will find activity guides, teaching materials, Web sites, and interpretive materials. Audio and interactive items, as well as written material, are also included. Educators can sign up for an e-mail newsletter, and public schoolteachers in New York state can borrow from an extensive collection of slides and videos.

**HIGHLIGHTS FOR TEACHERS:** The Red Studio area is directed at high school students. It includes an interactive design contest, interviews with artists, access to the museum's online projects, a neat tool for sending modern art e-cards to friends and family, and art resources chosen to appeal to teens.

Don't miss the **Online Guides** collection. Each of the three exhibitions encourages visitors to explore their perception and understanding of the full range of modern art. One exhibit covers the period from 1880 to 1920, another from 1920 to 1960, and the last from 1960 to the present.

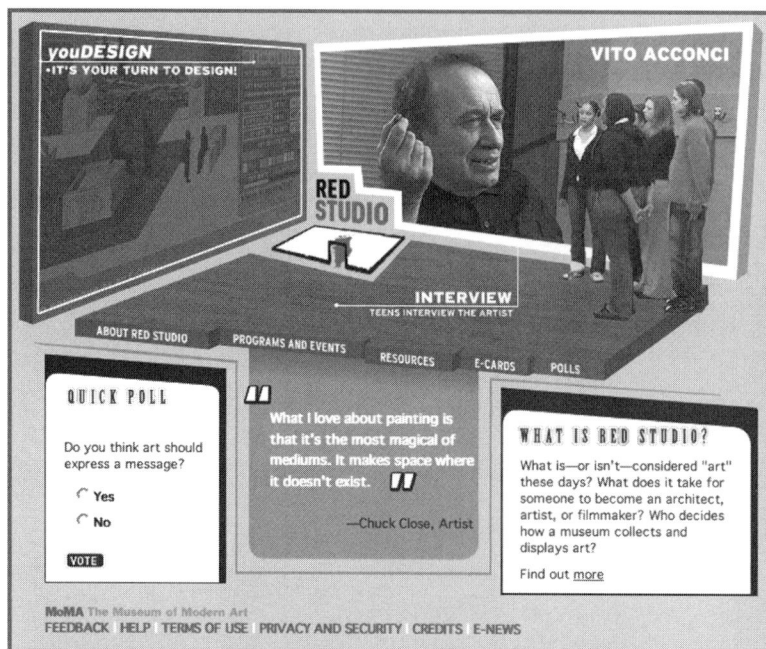

## National Gallery of Art: Education
www.nga.gov/education/education.htm

**SITE DESCRIPTION:** The National Gallery of Art (NGA) has teaching resources that can't be beat for quantity, quality, and thoughtfulness. Start with the dazzling **NGA Classroom** and **NGA Loan Program**. Then, scroll over to the column of hot buttons to the left of the vertical blue line. For online visitors, the sections titled **The Collection**, **Exhibitions**, **Online Tours**, and **NGA Kids** offer truly outstanding viewing and learning experiences. Throughout this site, most of the images of artwork can be enlarged, and selected areas may be inspected in detail.

The National Gallery of Art in Washington, D.C., "houses one of the finest collections in the world illustrating major achievements in painting, sculpture, decorative arts, and works on paper from the Middle Ages to the present."

**HIGHLIGHTS FOR TEACHERS:** The quality and quantity of educational resources at this site are truly astonishing. Within **NGA Classroom**, the **Featured Lessons** section helps learners explore art and origin myths, heroes and heroines, ecology, and 19th-century America through compilations that include **Discussion**, **Activities**, **Printables**, **Related Resources**, and a **Glossary**. Using the **Resource Finder**, teachers can search for materials in six curriculum areas, covering more than 35 topics and featuring nearly 60 artists. The **NGA Loan Program** is particularly outstanding: slide sets, multimedia programs, videos, CDs, DVDs, and resource guides can be borrowed for free! All you need to pay is return postage.

Don't miss **NGA Kids**. Despite the name, this area is not just for small fry. The page starts with 10 Adventures with Art—activities and projects in areas such as the senses, Native Americans, the quest for immortality, and more. There's also a link to **The Art Zone**, where visitors can create interactive art pieces using a variety of such online tools as Collage Machine, Pixel-Face, and 3-D Twirler. Other sites might have one or two places where you can create your own art online—the NGA has nine!

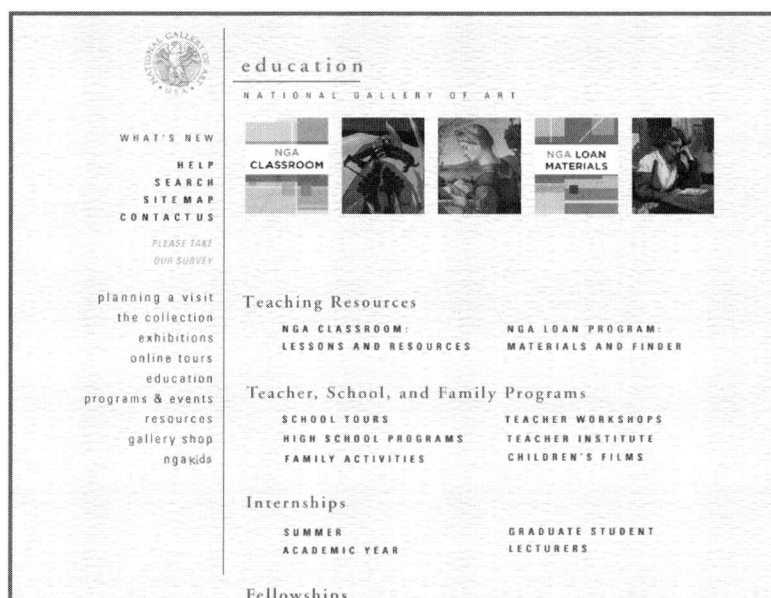

## TeachingArts.org

### www.teachingarts.org

**SITE DESCRIPTION:** TeachingArts.org focuses on teaching students about the arts: dance, music, theater, and visual arts. These four art forms are featured in their own tabbed sections, each of which offers subsections devoted to **Advocacy**, **Career Planning**, **Current Information**, **General Resources**, **Model Programs**, **Professional Development**, **Standards—Assessment**, and a discussion group.

The TeachingArts.org home page also includes access to the **Arts Center** by means of a link on the left. The Arts Center houses exhibits and online performance videos for all four of the art forms. **Interest Groups** hosts two organizations devoted to program assessment in the arts and also gives samples of model programs in the visual and performing arts.

**HIGHLIGHTS FOR TEACHERS:** For each of the four art forms, the areas most useful to teachers will probably be General Resources and Model Programs. Visitors will find described here organizations, programs, and sites from all over the United States. Each art form addresses general education students as well as English language learners and special populations. Under the Model Programs title, check out **Technology in the Arts** for some fabulously interesting Web sites!

For me, the pièce de résistance of this site is located in the Joy2Learn area. Clicking on the **Joy2Learn** logo takes you to a brilliant multimedia survey of the history and styles of tap dance, presented by Gregory Hines. It contains great film clips of the best tap dancers of the 20th century, demonstrations by Mr. Hines, and rich history of the dance. The video was taped shortly before his death; it's passionate, warm, witty, and wise.

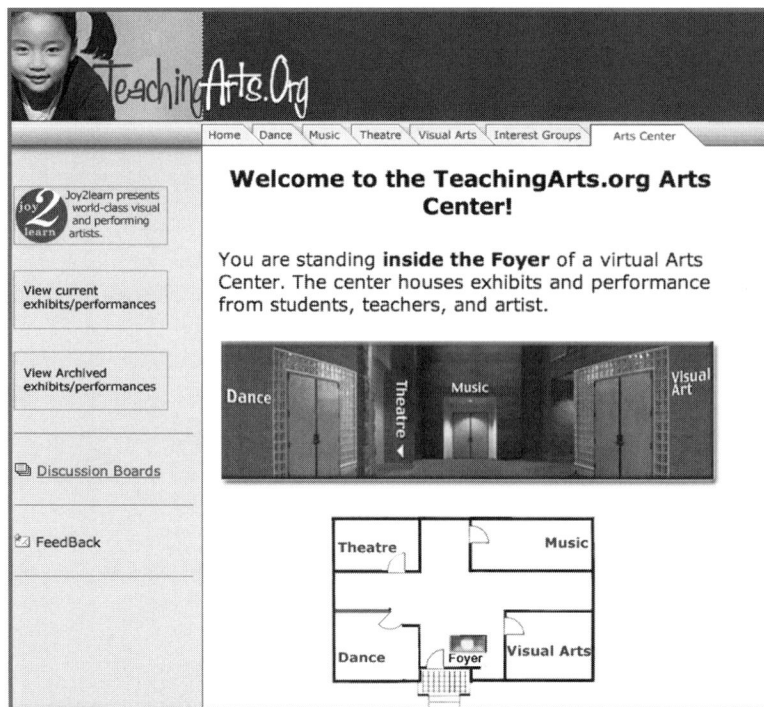

# CHAPTER 2

# College and Career Planning

The sites listed in this chapter contain powerful resources to help young adults plan and prepare for the future. The Career Key and O*NET furnish free career and personality assessments. In the case of The Career Key, they can be taken online and scored immediately. At the Vocational Information Center, visitors will encounter the most complete compilation of career, vocational, and technical education resources available on the Web.

For college-bound students, FastWeb, Peterson's, and College Board are a terrific trio. FastWeb is the best place to go for free information about scholarships. Peterson's provides comprehensive background information on schools and tips for writing those pesky admissions essays. College Board offers an abundance of information and samples to help students prepare for the SAT and related subject-area tests.

The New York Times Learning Network appears in this chapter because (among the many other great things found on this site) regular visitors are greeted with a Test Prep Question of the Day and a Word of the Day. Teachers will want to explore the wonderful lesson plans and go on multimedia Web Explorer tours on this site.

Last, but most definitely not least, SparkNotes offers free, online versions of the popular study guides sold in Barnes & Noble bookstores. Topics include literature, math, history, chemistry, biology, and physics. You'll find free SAT and ACT test prep here, as well as SparkNotes' very own "SAT novels." Each of these well-told tales contains the 1,000 vocabulary words most commonly found on the SAT.

# QUICK REFERENCE CHART

| College and Career Planning / Name of Site/URL | FEATURES FOR TEACHERS | | | | | | |
|---|---|---|---|---|---|---|---|
| | chat or forum | lesson plans | teacher resources | parent resources | teacher's guide | video, audio, applets | Web links |
| **The Career Key: Choosing a Career** www.careerkey.org | | | ■ | ■ | | | |
| **College Board** www.collegeboard.com | | ■ | ■ | ■ | ■ | ■ | ■ |
| **FastWeb** fastweb.monster.com | | ■ | ■ | ■ | ■ | ■ | ■ |
| **The New York Times Learning Network** www.nytimes.com/learning/ | | ■ | ■ | ■ | ■ | ■ | ■ |
| **O*NET Career Exploration Tools** www.onetcenter.org/tools.html | | ■ | ■ | ■ | ■ | ■ | ■ |
| **Peterson's** www.petersons.com | | ■ | ■ | ■ | ■ | ■ | ■ |
| **SparkNotes** sparknotes.com | ■ | ■ | ■ | ■ | ■ | ■ | ■ |
| **Vocational Information Center** www.khake.com | ■ | ■ | ■ | ■ | ■ | ■ | ■ |

The shaded boxes indicate the feature is available on the Web site.

## QUICK REFERENCE CHART *(continued)*

| College and Career Planning | FEATURES FOR TEACHERS | | | FEATURES FOR STUDENTS | | |
|---|---|---|---|---|---|---|
| **Name of Site/URL** | assessment ideas | e-newsletter | reproducibles | activities | interactive exercises | reading material |
| **The Career Key: Choosing a Career** www.careerkey.org | | | | | | |
| **College Board** www.collegeboard.com | | | | | | |
| **FastWeb** fastweb.monster.com | | | | | | |
| **The New York Times Learning Network** www.nytimes.com/learning/ | | | | | | |
| **O*NET Career Exploration Tools** www.onetcenter.org/tools.html | | | | | | |
| **Peterson's** www.petersons.com | | | | | | |
| **SparkNotes** sparknotes.com | | | | | | |
| **Vocational Information Center** www.khake.com | | | | | | |

The shaded boxes indicate the feature is available on the Web site.

## The Career Key: Choosing a Career
www.careerkey.org

**SITE DESCRIPTION:** Lawrence K. Jones, professor emeritus of the College of Education at North Carolina State University, originally published The Career Key back in 1987 to help students plan a career path. This site appeared on the Web in 1997, and it's now visited by more than 5,000 people each day. Both the site and the Career Key assessment are free of charge. They're intended for use by career planners ranging in age from middle school to adult.

The Career Key's centerpiece is the assessment exercise, which takes about 10 minutes to complete. Unlike many assessments on the Web, the Career Key is a professional-quality career test with demonstrated validity and benefits. The user's answers are automatically scored, and the results are linked to the federal *Occupational Outlook Handbook*. Hundred of schools, colleges, libraries, and agencies link to The Career Key, which is available in English, Chinese, and Korean (plans are underway to add other languages). Additional support materials are available for downloading at a nominal fee.

The Career Key is based on the ideas of counseling psychologist John L. Holland, whose work is briefly summarized on the site. Mr. Holland's basic premise is that people are generally one of six personality types in our culture, and those types can be linked to six ideal work environments. The personality types and work environments are given the same names: realistic, investigative, artistic, social, enterprising, and conventional.

**HIGHLIGHTS FOR TEACHERS:** After receiving their results from the Career Key assessment, visitors are encouraged to identify their job skills and continue to another section to obtain career help from the site. The site's career guidance system includes more than 20 self-help modules that represent the best practices and resources in the field. Titled Your Choices . . . , this section isn't directly accessible from the home page. Instead, click on **Continue** on the home page, and then click on the words **Get career help on topics like . . .** on the page that follows.

# College Board

www.collegeboard.com

**SITE DESCRIPTION:** Applying to college and taking the standardized college entrance exams is a rite of passage for American teenagers and their families. The College Board serves as one of the major gatekeepers, so it's important to know what this Web site has to say. The site offers a wide variety of free information for students, parents, and educators (along with plenty of fee-based products and services), ranging from test prep books for students to financial planning guides for parents and professional development for teachers and curriculum specialists.

As you would expect, visitors can sign up to take SAT and SAT-related tests online and also search for colleges of interest. The site supplies a personalized organizer to help students schedule and plan their test preparation. It also offers calendars and planning guidance for sophomores, juniors, and seniors. Students will find additional support for the college application process, including how to obtain financial aid. Free sample test questions, a full-length test, and a 68-question mini-SAT are located in the SAT Preparation Center. Click **For Students** and follow the links to the new SAT.

Students may also be interested in the **MyRoad** college and career planning area (**www. collegeboard.com/myroad/**). It offers a personality assessment to help match students to majors, careers, and colleges likely to suit them. Many schools and districts purchase this service for their students; individuals may buy in for $19.95 a year. Parents can find information on all of the same topics, written for their point of view. Nearly all information on the College Board site is available in Spanish as well as English.

**HIGHLIGHTS FOR TEACHERS:** Students in the class of 2006 face a new SAT, which replaces the previous test. On this site, educators will find extensive information about the new test, along with sample questions. Other remarkable services include the SAT Readiness Program, the AP Potential Program, professional development opportunities, and guidance on mapping a school's academic program to the requirements of the new SAT. Educators will be interested in the CollegeEd program, a free 12-lesson course designed to inspire students and their families to prepare for college (**www.collegeboard.com/collegeed/**).

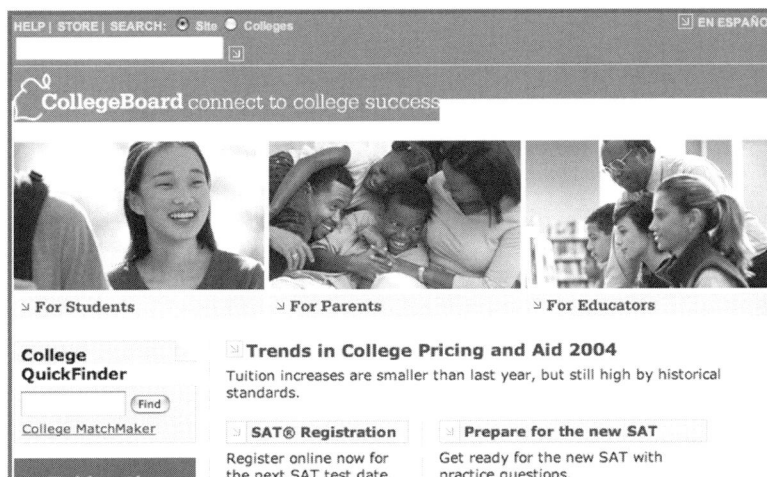

## FastWeb

**fastweb.monster.com**

**SITE DESCRIPTION:** FastWeb focuses on college scholarship information and college/applicant matching. As the oldest and most popular free online scholarship matching service, FastWeb was used by one-third of all college-bound seniors in 2003, and more than 21 million students have used it since 1995. The site is operated by Monster.com.

Visitors must register to use either the scholarship search or the college search. To match students to scholarships and colleges in a meaningful way, FastWeb asks registrants to supply considerable information. More than 600,000 scholarships (worth more than $1 billion) are listed on FastWeb, and more than 4,000 colleges recruit students through the site. More than 14,000 high schools have also joined.

FastWeb offers articles of interest to college-bound students on subjects such as **Admissions, Scholarships, Jobs, Financial Aid, Career Planning,** and **Money/College Life.** There's also a **Life After College Guide**, and tools such as a **Student Loan Payment Calculator**, a **College Cost Projector**, a **Budget Worksheet**, and **ACT/SAT Test Prep.**

As a free site, FastWeb is supported by advertisements and by selling, to selected marketers, registrant information. Registrants can opt to keep a lot of their information private, but not all of it.

**HIGHLIGHTS FOR TEACHERS:** When all is said and done, FastWeb does a solid job of matching students with scholarship information. To access the articles and tools, click on **Educators** at the bottom of any page; and when a new page opens, click on **Articles, Tools & More** at the top of the page, just under the FastWeb logo.

## The New York Times Learning Network
**www.nytimes.com/learning/**

**SITE DESCRIPTION:** What, you may ask, is the *New York Times* doing in the "College and Career Planning" chapter of this book? You may already know about the *Times'* daily **News Summaries** for students, the **Daily News Quiz**, the **Web Explorer** multimedia Internet tours, the **Science Q & A** section, the online student **Letters to the Editor**, the **Ask a Reporter** feature, and the **Web Navigator** guide to hot links all over the Internet in major curricular areas. But what do all these wonderful things have to do with college and career planning?

Well, this Web site also contains a **Test Prep Question of the Day** and a **Word of the Day**, both targeted at students preparing for the SAT. In addition, it hosts a wonderful collection of tools to increase knowledge. Throughout the **Student Connections** area of the site, readers can activate vocabulary and geography tools, which turn important vocabulary words blue and named geographic locations green, making each one a link to a dictionary definition of the word or a map depicting the location.

**HIGHLIGHTS FOR TEACHERS:** This site features, in **Teacher Connections**, great resources for teachers as well. The best of them is probably the **Daily Lesson Plan**, keyed to timely news topics and correlated to relevant educational standards. Developed in collaboration with Bank Street College, these lesson plans are archived and easily searchable. Don't miss the **Issues in Depth** news packages focused on important current and historic issues, all rich in resources such as lesson plans, quizzes, questionnaires, slideshows, crosswords, and historic *Times* articles.

The **Teacher Connections** section also carries, twice a month, a new, themed **Crossword Puzzle**. They're archived into 14 different subject areas for easy reference and can either be solved online or printed out. You'll also find an area titled **On This Day in History**, another featuring **Education News**, and a **Campus Webline**, which shows interested teachers and students how to publish an online newspaper for their school. Everything on this site is free.

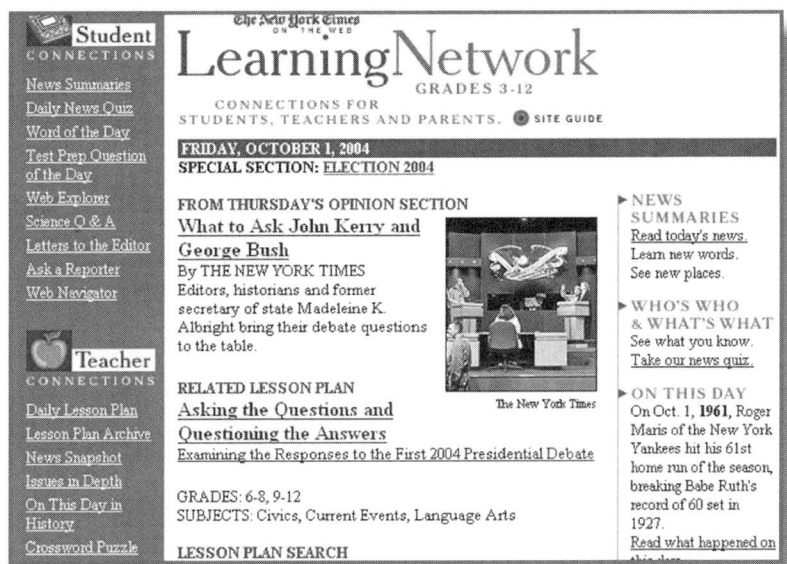

## O*NET Career Exploration Tools

www.onetcenter.org/tools.html

**SITE DESCRIPTION:** O*NET serves as "the nation's primary source of occupational information," replacing the well-known *Dictionary of Occupational Titles* with O*NET OnLine. The site serves multiple constituencies, including job seekers, job changers, students, career counselors, human resources practitioners, workers, education and training developers, program planners, policy makers, and educators.

The O*NET site provides **Career Exploration Tools**, the **O*NET OnLine** database, **Testing & Assessment Guides** for consumers, and the O*NET **Occupational Listings**. O*NET is an excellent starting place for students and adults looking for guidance regarding career planning.

**HIGHLIGHTS FOR TEACHERS:** High school teachers and counselors will probably find **Career Exploration Tools** and **Occupational Listings** to be the two most practical areas of this wide-ranging site. The site's five tools are designed to identify work-related interests, what users consider important on the job, and existing skills and abilities. All materials can be downloaded for free or purchased in bulk.

# Peterson's

**www.petersons.com**

**SITE DESCRIPTION:** Thomson Peterson's has long been known as one of the premier sources of information about postsecondary education, and this Web site offers a solid place to begin researching colleges and universities. Included are descriptions of four-year undergraduate programs, graduate and professional schools, two-year colleges, trade and technical schools, study abroad, executive education, distance education, private secondary schools, and summer programs for high school students. The well-designed site search engine makes it easy to identify programs that fit a searcher's individual profile.

Extensive information is also available on financial aid, the college application process, test preparation, and career services. Peterson's is a business, of course, and many of their services come with a price tag; but in many cases—such as the purchase of college test preparation materials for less than $20—sticker shock isn't much of a problem. The company even publishes prep books for the high school graduation tests now required by dozens of states in the United States, selling them for less than $15 each.

**HIGHLIGHTS FOR TEACHERS:** Peterson's supplements its information and search services with a lot of additional free support. Visitors can browse the topics listed in the vertical menu on the left-hand side of the home page. Clicking on one of these topics will take you to a new window, where you can find numerous free articles and resources as well as materials for sale.

In the **Test Preparation** area, visitors will find free mini-tests and test-taking tips as well as strategies for an alphabet soup of national standardized tests (SAT, ACT, PSAT, CLEP, TOEFL, AP, PCAT, etc.). Perhaps the best free materials on the site are the helpful tutorials on writing admissions essays. Click on **Admissions Essay Help** under **Apply to Colleges** in the left-hand menu. Click on the **Essay Tips & Samples** tab at the top of the EssayEdge page. You'll encounter a free, six-lesson course on writing an essay, along with more than a dozen examples of both well-done and poor essays.

## SparkNotes

**sparknotes.com**

**SITE DESCRIPTION:** SparkNotes is the Internet generation's answer to Cliff's Notes, which so many of us grew up and graduated with. Now, just-in-time students can easily find that last-minute study guide for the midterm exam—online and for free! Study guides are offered for the popular subjects **Literature**, **Drama**, **Philosophy**, **Poetry**, **Film**, and **Shakespeare**, and also for hundreds of other topics in **Math**, **History**, **Biography**, **Chemistry**, **Physics**, and **Biology**. The site also provides searchable prep books for the SAT, ACT, SAT II, and **The New SAT**. You get the same content as the SparkNotes books sold at Barnes & Noble, along with a practice test for each title, all gratis.

**HIGHLIGHTS FOR TEACHERS:** Besides the excellent summaries and study guides, you'll find nearly 150 full-text versions of classical literature, poetry, drama, and philosophy. You'll also find hundreds of online message boards where students discuss the literature they're reading and other subjects they're studying. In addition, there's a reference section containing a Merriam-Webster's dictionary, a thesaurus, a calculator, and a foreign language translator for six languages. If you register, you can take dozens of serious and frivolous psychological and personality tests, and also start your own blog. SparkNotes has recently partnered with FastWeb, so SparkNotes users now have direct access to all of FastWeb's scholarship information.

The final piece to this excellent Web site are the unique "SAT novels," available to visitors who register for SparkLife. Each well-told tale contains all of the 1,000 most common words on the SAT, with target words highlighted and hyperlinked to full dictionary definitions. New chapters are added each week. This site is an inexhaustible resource for busy high school students!

# Vocational Information Center

**www.khake.com**

**SITE DESCRIPTION:** Kathryn Hake is a retired vocational educator who has successfully created a Web site that no think tank, university, foundation, or government agency has been able to match in breadth or depth. She's gathered an amazing amount of career, vocational, and technical information, organized it, and put it on the Internet so that all interested parties can easily find what they want.

Content is king on this site, so there are no graphics (a big help to visitors who access the site using a slow dial-up connection). Resources are neatly organized into categorical lists. The Vocational Information Center is searchable and also carries a thorough index and site map. More than 200 schools, libraries, articles, texts, organizations, and Web sites have chosen to link themselves to this site.

**HIGHLIGHTS FOR TEACHERS:** Ms. Hake's home page lists nearly 100 categories of Career and Technical Education Web Resources, including **Academics**, **Agriculture**, **Electronics**, **Health**, **Masonry**, **Plumbing**, **Safety**, **Transportation**, and **Welding**. A visit to the **Site Map** makes it easy to find information about Career Exploration; Skills; Schools; Job Market; Educators; Reference; Search Engines; and Images, Clip Art and Photographs.

## VOCATIONAL INFORMATION CENTER

Explore vocational and technical careers, check out the skills employers really want, find a trade school, research technical topics and take a look at the current job market within the

**Vocational Information Center**

### Career and Technical Education Web Resources

| | | | | |
|---|---|---|---|---|
| Academics | College Planning | Food Science | Manufacturing | Schools by State |
| Agriculture | Communication | Graphic Arts | Masonry | Schools by Trade |
| Animals | Skills | Guidance | Math | Science |
| Apprenticeships | Computer / IT | Health | Metal Working | Search Engines |
| Arts | Cosmetology | History and | Military | Security and |
| Auto Body | CTE State | Geography | Nursing | Protective |
| Automotive | Resources | Horticulture | Occupational | Site Map |
| Aviation & | Culinary | HVACR | Licensure | Skills |
| Aerospace | Data and Statistics | Images | Painting & Repair | Standards |
| Broadcast Media | Diseases | Index to Site | Pennsylvania | Standards - |
| Business | Educators | Inventors and | Performing Arts | Vocational |
| Career | Electrical | Inventions | Photography and | Teacher Resources |
| Curriculum | Electronics | Job Market | Film | Telecommunications |
| Career | Energy/Power | Journalism | Plumbing | Tutorial Resources |
| Descriptions | Engine Technology | Law Enforcement | Printing | Transportation |
| Career | Engineering | Landscape Design | Reference | Visual Arts |
| Exploration | English/LA | Lesson Plans - | Safety | Vocational |
| Career Planning | Entrepreneur | General | Scholarships / Aid | Education |
| Carpentry | Environment | Lesson Plans - | Schools | Vocational Teacher |
| Child Care | | Vocational | | Welding |
| Clipart | | Machining | | |

·Home  ·Careers  ·Skills  ·Schools  ·Job Market  ·Educators  ·Reference
·Search  ·Academics  ·Clip Art
·Inventors  ·Tutorials  ·Pennsylvania  ·Safety  ·Diseases  ·Index  ·About  ·Site Map

**VOCATIONAL**
INFORMATION CENTER

Last updated: Wednesday,
Feb 18, 2004
URL: http://www.khake.com

# CHAPTER 3

# English

The Web sites selected for this chapter will go a long way toward lightening the load for English teachers. The sites W. W. Norton & Company and American Literature on the Web do an excellent job of helping readers understand the literary and historical context of what they're reading. The Moonlit Road contains both audio and written versions of wonderful ghost stories and folktales from the American South. Meanwhile, audio and written versions of great poems—along with unit and lesson plans that build on them—can be found at Online Poetry Classroom.

English Language and Literature Resources, Outta Ray's Head, and Web English Teacher are excellent general reference sites for English teachers. Writing teachers will find valuable Teaching That Makes Sense and Purdue University's Online Writing Lab. Meeting the Secondary Reading Challenge is host to a fabulous collection of video clips, resources, and best practices focused on helping secondary-level students read better and more effectively. Media Literacy Clearinghouse aptly describes itself as one-stop shopping for just about anything you might want to learn about media literacy. When it comes to innovative applications of technology in the English classroom, John F. Barber, Ph. D., and Cyber English are full of world-class ideas.

Finally, for those involved in journalism, High School Journalism links to more than 500 high school and middle school student newspapers (both hard-copy and online versions). It guides students and teachers through the process of publishing a paper. The Write Site devotes itself to helping middle school students and teachers publish papers for their schools.

# QUICK REFERENCE CHART

| English | FEATURES FOR TEACHERS | | | | | | |
|---|---|---|---|---|---|---|---|
| **Name of Site/URL** | chat or forum | lesson plans | teacher resources | parent resources | teacher's guide | video, audio, applets | Web links |
| **American Literature on the Web** www.nagasaki-gaigo.ac.jp/ishikawa/amlit/ | | | | | | | |
| **Cyber English** www.tnellen.com/cybereng/ | | | | | | | |
| **English Language and Literature Resources** dewey.chs.chico.k12.ca.us/engl.html | | | | | | | |
| **High School Journalism** highschooljournalism.org | | | | | | | |
| **John F. Barber, Ph.D.** www.brautigan.net/john | | | | | | | |
| **Media Literacy Clearinghouse** medialit.med.sc.edu | | | | | | | |
| **Meeting the Secondary Reading Challenge** www.sarasota.k12.fl.us/sarasota/mainmenu.htm | | | | | | | |
| **The Moonlit Road** www.themoonlitroad.com | | | | | | | |
| **Online Poetry Classroom** www.onlinepoetryclassroom.org | | | | | | | |
| **Online Writing Lab, Purdue University** owl.english.purdue.edu | | | | | | | |
| **Outta Ray's Head: Lesson Plans, Handouts, and Ideas** home.cogeco.ca/~rayser3 | | | | | | | |
| **Teaching That Makes Sense** www.ttms.org | | | | | | | |
| **Web English Teacher** www.webenglishteacher.com | | | | | | | |
| **The Write Site** www.writesite.org | | | | | | | |
| **W. W. Norton & Company: Student Resources** www.wwnorton.com/college/titles/students/ | | | | | | | |

The shaded boxes indicate the feature is available on the Web site.

# QUICK REFERENCE CHART *(continued)*

| English<br><br>Name of Site/URL | FEATURES FOR TEACHERS | | | FEATURES FOR STUDENTS | | |
|---|---|---|---|---|---|---|
| | assessment ideas | e-newsletter | reproducibles | activities | interactive exercises | reading material |
| **American Literature on the Web**<br>www.nagasaki-gaigo.ac.jp/ishikawa/amlit/ | | | | | | |
| **Cyber English**<br>www.tnellen.com/cybereng/ | | | | | | |
| **English Language and Literature Resources**<br>dewey.chs.chico.k12.ca.us/engl.html | | | | | | |
| **High School Journalism**<br>highschooljournalism.org | | | | | | |
| **John F. Barber, Ph.D.**<br>www.brautigan.net/john | | | | | | |
| **Media Literacy Clearinghouse**<br>medialit.med.sc.edu | | | | | | |
| **Meeting the Secondary Reading Challenge**<br>www.sarasota.k12.fl.us/sarasota/mainmenu.htm | | | | | | |
| **The Moonlit Road**<br>www.themoonlitroad.com | | | | | | |
| **Online Poetry Classroom**<br>www.onlinepoetryclassroom.org | | *Online Poetry Classroom Bulletin* | | | | |
| **Online Writing Lab, Purdue University**<br>owl.english.purdue.edu | | *Purdue OWL News* | | | | |
| **Outta Ray's Head: Lesson Plans, Handouts, and Ideas**<br>home.cogeco.ca/~rayser3 | | | | | | |
| **Teaching That Makes Sense**<br>www.ttms.org | | | | | | |
| **Web English Teacher**<br>www.webenglishteacher.com | | | | | | |
| **The Write Site**<br>www.writesite.org | | | | | | |
| **W. W. Norton & Company: Student Resources**<br>www.wwnorton.com/college/titles/students/ | | | | | | |

The shaded boxes indicate the feature is available on the Web site.

## American Literature on the Web

www.nagasaki-gaigo.ac.jp/ishikawa/amlit/

**SITE DESCRIPTION:** This marvelous site is maintained by Akihito Ishikawa of the Department of English at Nagasaki University of Foreign Studies in Japan. It's both wonderful and ironic that such an outstanding resource on America literature comes from Nagasaki.

Professor Ishikawa has organized the site in a straightforward manner. The first major category, General Resources: American Literature, contains materials on **Movements & Genre**, **Poetry**, **Drama**, **Literary Theory**, and other literary topics. The second category, General Resources: Arts and Humanities, includes material on **American Studies**, **U.S. History** and **Scholarly Societies**, and has various other interdisciplinary links. The site also contains a well-designed historical index of American literature that groups works and authors into periods. Within each period, you can search through **Timelines**, **Authors**, **Related Resources**, **Music & Visual Arts**, and **Social Contexts**. Nearly 150 colleges, libraries, and other Web sites from around the world link themselves to American Literature on the Web.

**HIGHLIGHTS FOR TEACHERS:** The single most outstanding resource available here is the historical index. It provides a wonderful collection of materials that can help educators and students situate a literary work within the culture of its time, encouraging a deeper and richer understanding of the work and its potential interpretations. One caveat: the site is still incomplete, as if the professor has stepped out of the classroom before quite finishing his lecture. One hopes the professor will return someday to close the loop on this great project.

### American Literature Resources in Section by Period

○ Browse American Literature Resources in Section by Period:

| Periods | Timelines | Authors | Related Resources | Visual Arts | Social Contexts |
|---------|-----------|---------|-------------------|-------------|-----------------|
| Contents **(1620-1820)** | Timelines | Authors (frame) | Related Resources | Music & Visual Arts | Social Contexts |
| Contents **(1820-1865)** | Timelines | Authors (frame) | Related Resources | Music & Visual Arts | Social Contexts |
| Contents **(1865-1914)** | Timelines | Authors (frame) | Related Resources | Music & Visual Arts | Social Contexts |
| Contents **(1914-1945)** | Timelines | Authors (frame) | Related Resources | Music & Visual Arts | Social Contexts |
| Contents **(Since 1945)** | Timelines | Authors (frame) | Related Resources | Music & Visual Arts | Social Contexts |

○ Browse Complete Alphabetical Listing of American Authors (frame)
○ Browse Complete Alphabetical Listing of American Authors (no frame)
○ Browse Complete Alphabetical Listing of American Authors : Japanese Resources pages (frame)
○ Browse Complete Alphabetical Listing of American Authors : Japanese Resources pages (no frame)

[ Search AmLit on The Web ]　[ Search the Net ]

## Cyber English

**www.tnellen.com/cybereng/**

**www.tnellen.com/school/cylib.html**

**SITE DESCRIPTION:** You may wonder why two URLs are listed for this site. That's because Cyber English, the brainchild of Ted Nellen, is such a glorious, untidy accumulation of sites and sounds that it has spread inexorably from its original Web address to an associated site. Materials collected five or six years ago mingle with things just posted yesterday. Ideas are piled upon proposals, while hotlists rub shoulders with lengthy articles.

Consequently, it's pretty hard to navigate through this site with any set of linear expectations. The two points of entry listed above are the most obvious places to begin.

**HIGHLIGHTS FOR TEACHERS:** Scores of links are provided on these two main sites, listed in no particular order but usefully titled and highlighted. Surf to whatever piques your curiosity. At many points, you'll see the name Ted Nellen printed in color, meaning that it's hyperlinked. Click on it and spend a little time reading his resumé: the recounting of his experiences as a college English teacher helps explain his philosophy for the Web site. Likewise, the descriptions and materials from his years as a high school teacher and his short stint in the school district's office yield plenty of practical advice.

## Cyber English

### The Practice

by

**Ted Nellen**

*I hear and I forget*
*I see and I remember*
*I do and I understand*

Ancient Chinese Proverb
&
An Educational Aphorism

**Cyber English.....** Taught by **Ted Nellen**
The Work of the Information Technology HS **Scholars** 2003-
The Work of the Alternative HS **Scholars** 2000-2003
The Work of the Bergtraum **Scholars** 1994-2000

**See & Read**

**The Web-Book** *The Theory*

## English Language and Literature Resources

dewey.chs.chico.k12.ca.us/engl.html

**SITE DESCRIPTION:** English Language and Literature Resources is offered by Chico High School in California—in particular, the school library and its Webmaster, Peter Milbury. The site consists of an excellent collection of well-chosen links for high school English teachers. The home page starts with general information, including research assignment resources that teachers have created for projects and courses of study at Chico High School.

The rest of the Web site consists of a list of selected Web resources, each briefly described. They're grouped into categories, including Book Reviews and Criticism; Drama Resources; Mythology, Folklore, Medieval, and Classical Literature; Poetry, Poetry Archives, and Collections; Philosophy and Philosophers; and Shakespearean England. The site also includes **English As A Second Language** links.

**HIGHLIGHTS FOR TEACHERS:** Of the 110 links on the site, 32 address topics related to poetry, making it a particularly rich source of material for teaching this genre.

Besides English, the library's main page (**dewey.chs.chico.k12.ca.us/**) offers links to 26 other online subject collections from the Chico High School Library, each one as meticulously selected as English Language and Literature Resources. Every high school should have a library media specialist so energetic, diligent, and thorough as Peter Milbury. If you're a high school teacher (or student) looking for resources on the Internet, in any subject, the Chico High School Library is a terrific place to start.

## High School Journalism

**highschooljournalism.org**

**SITE DESCRIPTION:** This lively and engaging site offers abundant information about high school student journalism, careers in the field, links to hundreds of high school newspapers, and support for journalism teachers and high school newspaper advisers. It's divided into separate sections titled **Students**, **Teachers**, **Guidance** (scholarships, programs, and careers), and **Editors**. Each section contains large compilations of key articles and information sure to be of interest to site visitors. For example, the **Students** section features **Ask a Pro** (interviews with professional newspeople), online video clips of **Student Opinions**, skills tests, lists of journalism schools, scholarship information, and student journalism awards.

**HIGHLIGHTS FOR TEACHERS:** The **Teachers** section includes more than 200 **Lesson Plans** and dozens of **Teaching Tips** covering topics such as Advertising, Copy Editing, Design and Color, Diversity, Editorial Pages, Ethics, and Fundraising Ideas. The links to more than 350 high school newspapers (under **HS Newspapers**) are quite impressive. Even more striking is the **my. highschooljournalism.org** area, accessible on the bottom right-hand side of the home page. It consists of weekly news headlines from the best student journalists across the country. This area also hosts online newspapers from 293 high schools and 37 middle and elementary schools.

Don't miss the **Broadcast** area, accessible from the upper right-hand side of the home page. It focuses on high school broadcast journalism and informs visitors how broadcast stations and high schools can receive grants of up to $5,000 to create a new broadcast program or to foster a partnership between high schools and their local stations.

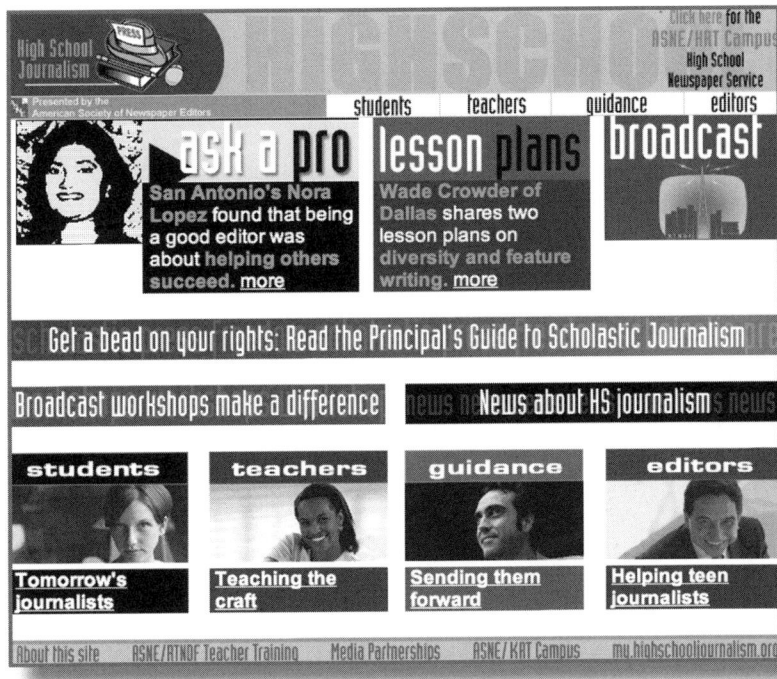

## John F. Barber, Ph.D.

**www.brautigan.net/john**

**SITE DESCRIPTION:** Dr. John Barber's Web site reveals that he's a man of significant academic accomplishment in technology, administration, and literature. His well-known Dr. John's Eazy-Peazy Guides (click on **E-Z Guides** under Projects) have been available on the Web since at least 1996 and are treasured by many for their intelligence, wit, creativity, and amalgamation of computer technology with the written word.

On the left-hand side of the home page is a convenient vertical frame listing topics such as Information, Projects, and Downloads. The topic labeled **Bored?** takes you to a page filled with games and pesky cyber-ants. A small word of caution: navigating through this site can be tricky. Many of the links take you to dead ends and 404 error messages. It can be a little frustrating at times, but it's well worth it when you find what you're looking for.

**HIGHLIGHTS FOR TEACHERS:** Five Eazy-Peazy Guides are offered: **Effective Writing**, **Creative** (Writing) **Ideas**, **HTML Coding**, **Research Skills**, and **Public Speaking**. Four of them are insightful, clearly conveyed roadmaps designed to help people simplify and focus their communication processes. The fifth guide—The Eazy-Peazy Guide to Creative (Writing) Ideas—is the standout. Dr. Barber has created nine "engines" designed to stimulate the creative process for writers of all ages. Mere words cannot do justice to these unique idea-generators, which go by the names **Essay Engine**, **Quote Engine**, **Prompt Engine**, **Fortune Engine**, **Buzzword Engine**, **Profundity Engine**, **Quip Engine**, **Names Engine**, and **Vocabulary Engine**. They combine computer technology with writing in an enormously clever fashion. You'll not regret the time you spend revving these engines!

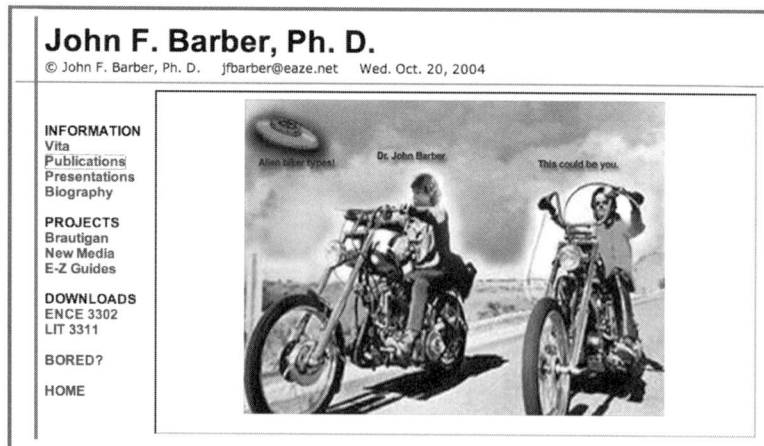

## Media Literacy Clearinghouse
### medialit.med.sc.edu

**SITE DESCRIPTION:** This Web site is aptly named. It succeeds in gathering under one "roof," for K–12 educators, the highest quality information now available on media literacy teaching and learning. Media Literacy Clearinghouse not only is a great resource for teachers and students, but it also serves to build public consciousness regarding the importance of media literacy to K–12 and higher education.

The site is organized into more than 50 topical subjects, such as **Advertising**, **Assessment**, **Body Image**, **Information Literacy**, **Math In The Media**, **Media Use Statistics**, **Politics In The Media**, **War Reporting**, and **Compare & Contrast** Two Versions of the Same News Story. Each subject provides articles, Web sites, and original source material.

**HIGHLIGHTS FOR TEACHERS:** Media Literacy Clearinghouse takes its commitment to standards-based education seriously, and the author has made a strong effort to connect media literacy issues with standards in reading, writing, science, math, and social studies. Teachers will likely find many of the topical subjects to be of interest. Examples include **Integrating Media Literacy into the Social Studies**, **Media Lit Resources for Addressing Media and Health**, **Math & Science Connections to Media Literacy**, and **Assessment**.

Check out a list of upcoming and past presentations made by the site's Webmaster, Frank Baker, at **medialit.med.sc.edu/presentations.htm**. You'll find a number of blue links embedded in the lengthy lists, some of which contain excellent PowerPoint presentations. They address aspects of media literacy, its importance to our society, and ways to teach it effectively.

## Meeting the Secondary Reading Challenge

**www.sarasota.k12.fl.us/sarasota/mainmenu.htm**

**SITE DESCRIPTION:** This is a wonderful Web site that manages to be practical and theoretical at the same time. It takes a feast of strategies, tips, and program descriptions and arranges them into bite-sized chunks that teachers will find easy to digest. The site also contains graphic organizers and video clips that illustrate and support many of its suggested best practices.

Another nice aspect of this site is that it models teaching in a technology-rich environment. While it starts off with a straightforward main menu page, visitors can choose to take any number of paths that lead to materials for **Reading Teachers**, **Content Area Teachers**, **Teachers of ESOL Students**, **Parents**, and **Students**. No matter which path they take, visitors will find a rich collection of articles, topics, and strategies, as well as links for deeper exploration.

**HIGHLIGHTS FOR TEACHERS:** One way to access the resources on this site is to jump to the **Best Practices** section, which includes pieces on **Interdisciplinary Instruction**, **Cooperative Learning**, **Creative & Critical Thinking**, **Constructivist Learning Environments**, **Multiple Intelligences**, **Authentic Assessment**, and **Implementing Technology**. These sections provide both a theoretical foundation upon which the practice is based and practical suggestions on how to implement it. The site also contains an excellent section on **FCAT**, the Florida Comprehensive Assessment Test, with many resources, strategies, and practice questions. Although your state's tests and standards may not be identical to Florida's, most of the underlying content on these tests is similar from state to state.

One of the most noteworthy sections on the site is **Reading Strategies That Assist in Content Area Reading** (under **Content Area Teachers**), which suggests nine specific practices. And don't miss the **Media Center**; it contains 18 **Video Clips** that show how to implement multiple intelligences, reciprocal teaching, and the nationally validated CRISS (Creating Independence through Student-Owned Strategies), for developing thoughtful and independent learners.

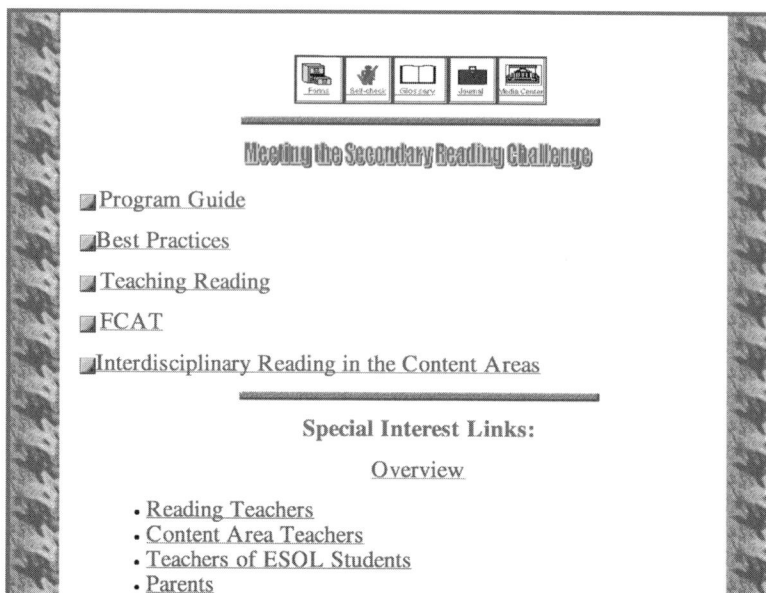

## The Moonlit Road

www.themoonlitroad.com

**SITE DESCRIPTION:** This site houses a terrific collection of Southern ghost stories and folktales, in both written and audio versions. Most stories are accompanied by background information about their origins, so readers can gain insight into the cultural roots of the American South.

A number of featured stories appear on the site several times per year—text versions that are accompanied by audio. A full archive is maintained for all text versions, but the archive contains no audio. Free registration is required to access the archive. The Moonlit Road also maintains five message boards for readers to interact with one another. A separate free registration is required to post messages to the boards.

**HIGHLIGHTS FOR TEACHERS:** The stories on The Moonlit Road are not for the very young, nor are they of the easy-reading variety. That's why the audio narrations, by accomplished storytellers, can be so important. Students who can understand the content, but may not be able to read the text fluently, will be able to read along as they listen.

The Moonlit Road also provides a list of links to more than 30 sites. These sites include more stories about Southern culture, storytelling, myths, folktales, and ghosts and other paranormal happenings.

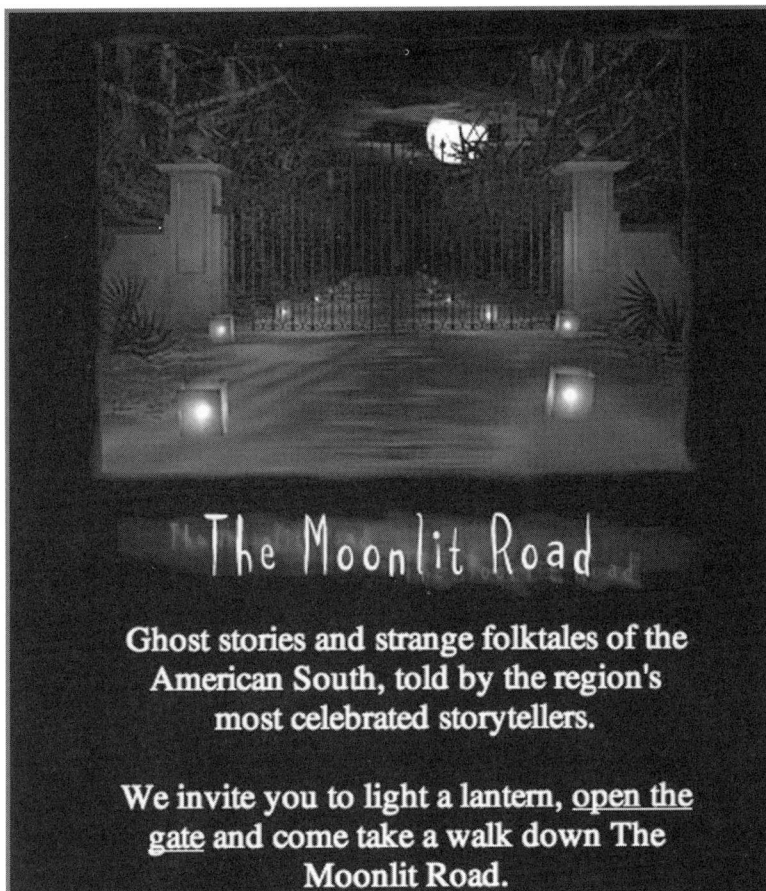

The Moonlit Road

Ghost stories and strange folktales of the American South, told by the region's most celebrated storytellers.

We invite you to light a lantern, open the gate and come take a walk down The Moonlit Road.

## Online Poetry Classroom

www.onlinepoetryclassroom.org

**SITE DESCRIPTION:** Online Poetry Classroom is produced by The Academy of American Poets to encourage the teaching and appreciation of poetry in the high school language arts curriculum. It's designed to operate as an "interactive professional development program and a virtual community enabling teachers across the country to access free poetry resources online." At press time, Online Poetry Classroom was in the process of being merged with the academy's main site, **Poets.org**.

The site is quite comprehensive, offering curriculum units, discussion forums, lesson plans, pedagogical and critical essays, teacher resources, teaching ideas and tip sheets, and links to state and district standards. The **Find a Poem** and **Find a Poet** areas offer access to more than 1,200 poems as well as biographical information about 450 poets. A nice search feature allows viewers to quickly look up poets (by state or name) and poems (by title, first line, or keyword).

**HIGHLIGHTS FOR TEACHERS:** For visitors who register, the site provides a notebook feature that allows you to save any linked item from the site, including poems, articles, and audio clips. Registration also enables you to participate in forum discussions. The excellent **What to Teach** area contains resources in categories such as **Great Poems to Teach**, **Curated Exhibits**, **National Poetry Map of America**, **Poetry Timeline**, **Media Center**, and **Committed to Memory**, which lists the 100 best poems to memorize. The **Media Center** includes audio clips of more than 100 poems and a link to the **Favorite Poem Project**, which houses nearly 50 video clips of Americans reciting their favorite poetry. Online Poetry Classroom contains extensive links to contemporary poets, teacher resources, and standards. It also publishes a free monthly e-mail newsletter for high school teachers.

# Online Writing Lab, Purdue University
## owl.english.purdue.edu

**SITE DESCRIPTION:** Purdue's Online Writing Lab (OWL) has gained an international reputation as a top resource for writing support for both instructors and students. The number of visitors to the site has grown from 3.6 million per year in 2000 to 23.3 million in 2003. Purdue's Online Writing Lab offers e-mail tutoring for brief questions and a free weekly e-mail newsletter.

The site is organized into four main sections that are easily accessed from drop-down lists at the top of the home page. One list gives information about the **Writing Lab and OWL**, another gives access to **Handouts and Materials** in nine categories, a third takes visitors to online **Workshops & Presentations** in nine categories, and the fourth to **Internet Resources** in five categories. The site is fully searchable.

**HIGHLIGHTS FOR TEACHERS:** New visitors should take the **virtual lab tour**, which introduces the site's wide variety of resources. There's considerable material for ESL teachers, too. Particularly helpful are both the material designed for teachers involved in Writing Across the Curriculum and the very selective set of **Internet Resources** for teachers, while the most popular parts of the site are likely to be the handouts and PowerPoint presentations. You're bound to find great material here for your language arts and English composition classroom.

## Outta Ray's Head: Lesson Plans, Handouts, and Ideas

home.cogeco.ca/~rayser3

**SITE DESCRIPTION:** There really is a Ray (and a head) behind this superb Web site. His name is Ray Saitz, and he describes himself as a "teacher/librarian in a small high school near Bowmanville, Ontario." Mr. Saitz became frustrated both by the lack of high school English lessons to be found on the Web in the mid-1990s and by the fact that those that did exist didn't have good handouts. So he set out to post his own lessons, complete with rationales, handouts, and evaluations.

The lesson plans are organized into five sections (click on **The Lessons**): **Literature**, **Poetry**, **Library**, **Writing**, and **Links**. Altogether, probably 250 separate resources can be found on this site. Additional material is added on a regular basis. Many teachers have contributed lessons to the collection, and each is acknowledged with gratitude.

**HIGHLIGHTS FOR TEACHERS:** Without a doubt, the highlights here are the great lesson plans. It's clear that Ray Saitz takes this work seriously, so anything included on his site has to meet his exacting standards. As he is proud of pointing out, "all of the lessons have been used and refined in the classroom." You can be sure that the 22 links he's selected are top-notch as well.

*Welcome to*

# Outta Ray's Head

*Lesson plans, handouts, and ideas.*

*A collection of lesson plans with handouts by Ray Saitz and many contributors; all of the lessons have been used and refined in the classroom.*

The Lessons

About the Site

About the Author

*Any handouts can be used by teachers without any fee; however, you should e-mail me or the original author to let me, or him, or her, know that you did.*

## Teaching That Makes Sense
**www.ttms.org**

**SITE DESCRIPTION:** Teaching That Makes Sense is all about writing. It approaches the subject from a serious and thoughtful point of view, presenting a wealth of print resources on a wide variety of topics. If you want to delve deeply into the teaching of writing, this site presents a plethora of theories, practical strategies, examples of student writing, and assessment schemes.

In all fairness to the Web site's developer, Steve Peha, it should be pointed out that the site offers a great deal of information about his company, Teaching That Makes Sense, Inc.—including its many products, services, and workshops for educators. All in all, however, this site contains an enormously rich collection of short books and articles, all free and downloadable.

**HIGHLIGHTS FOR TEACHERS:** The unquestionable highlight of Teaching That Makes Sense is the remarkable collection of short books on teaching writing that are available free for download. They range in length from 27 pages to 124 pages, with the average being about 50. Each one offers valuable insights and support. Titles include *The Writing Teacher's Strategy Guide*, *Prompted Writing*, *Student Writing Samples Grades K–12*, *An Introduction to the Writing Process*, *Welcome to Writer's Workshop*, *Writing Across the Curriculum*, *Writing Assessment*, *The Five Facts of Fiction*, *What Is Good Writing?*, *The Organizers*, and *The Reading-Writing Poster Pack*.

## Web English Teacher

www.webenglishteacher.com

**SITE DESCRIPTION:** Carla Beard founded Web English Teacher as a place to gather "the best of K–12 English/Language Arts teaching resources: lesson plans, WebQuests, videos, biography, e-texts, criticism, jokes, puzzles, and classroom activities." She's organized these Web-based resources into 22 categories and provides links and a brief description of each Web site.

**HIGHLIGHTS FOR TEACHERS:** Secondary teachers will find many useful activities, strategies, and materials in the sections titled **Critical Thinking**, **Drama**, **Journalism & Yearbook**, **Media & Media Literacy**, **Poetry**, **Speech & Debate**, and **Young Adult Fiction**. The Web sites collected here have been selected for their quality and usefulness. The descriptions are particularly helpful when trying to decide which of these resources will be of most value to you and your students.

The Alliance for Excellent Education and the Carnegie Corporation of New York recently released a report on adolescent literacy in the United States. It recommends 15 "essential components" of a successful reading program:

- Direct, explicit, comprehensive reading instruction
- Effective instructional principles embedded in conent
- Motivation and self-directed learning
- Text-based collaborative learning
- Strategic tutoring
- Diverse texts
- Intensive writing
- A technology component
- Ongoing formative assessment of students
- Extended time for literacy
- Professional development
- Ongoing summative assessment of students and programs
- Teacher teams
- Leadership
- A comprehensive and coordinated literacy program

## The Write Site

www.writesite.org

**SITE DESCRIPTION:** Teachers who want to get middle school students involved in a journalism project, or who want to launch a new or improved student newspaper, will find lots of help here. This Web site gives a brief history of journalism, outlines career opportunities, and gives links to professional and student news organizations. Students learn to perform online and in-library research as well as develop a personal writing style. Correlation to the state of Ohio's Test Proficiencies is also provided.

**HIGHLIGHTS FOR TEACHERS:** For teachers, the best place to go on this site is **Extra, Extra!!** To get there, from the splash page select **On the Inside**, then scroll down and click on **Editor's Desk**. Here, you'll find a complete instructional guide, specially designed **Graphic Organizers**, **Task Cards**, and **Checklists**—a complete package for teaching a well-executed unit. Visitors will encounter references to materials such as videos and computer software that were provided to the participant schools of the original project in Ohio, but most are no longer available. While it would be nice to have access to these supplemental materials, their absence does not diminish the great value to be found here.

**Editor's Desk**

FOR TEACHERS

You're in charge. You oversee everything that goes on in your classroom each day. And that's no easy task. You're always looking for good resources. Save time and energy right here by taking advantage of the links and materials at your fingertips on the EDITOR'S DESK.

**Stop the Presses** What's the breaking story?
Catch up on the latest developments in teaching language arts. Learn how to use technology in your classroom with these professional development links.

**Extra, Extra!!** Need teaching materials?
Download lesson descriptions, task cards, graphic organizers, and checklists for classroom activities.

HOME  BACK  NEWSROOM  NEWSSTAND

## W. W. Norton & Company: Student Resources

www.wwnorton.com/college/titles/students/

**SITE DESCRIPTION:** W. W. Norton publishes textbooks, primarily college textbooks, on numerous subjects. This Web site contains material that supports a great many of these publications. Language arts teachers should click on English in the list titled Select a Discipline. You'll be taken to a window that contains links to *The Norton Anthology of American Literature, The Norton Anthology of English Literature, The Norton Anthology of World Literature, The Norton Introduction to Literature/Poetry, The Norton Sampler, The Norton Reader,* and *Picturing Texts.* In the listing for each of these volumes, visitors can find supporting resources by clicking on the links titled **Student Web Site, Norton Topics Online, Norton Online Archive,** or **Litweb.**

The textbooks named above are widely used in colleges and universities throughout the world. What's terrific about this site is that W. W. Norton provides extensive support material for students, and much of the literature that students read in high school is drawn from the same canon they will encounter in college. Obviously, to get the most benefit from this site, students should be reading the same texts that appear in the anthologies. Fortunately, many of them are available for free at such sites as Project Gutenberg, Bartleby, and the Internet Public Library.

The student support materials consist of outlines and summaries, timelines with historical and literary contexts, explorations that help students dig deeper into their reading and draw connections, topical articles, links to related sites, maps, and more. One caveat: the Web site appears to limit the number of times visitors may freely access any specific support site in a single online session; you may have to visit more than once.

**HIGHLIGHTS FOR TEACHERS:** *The Norton Anthology of American Literature* is supported by an outstanding companion Web site, American Passages, located on the Annenberg/CPB site (**www.learner.org/resources/series164.html**). These resources are in addition to the already extensive student materials mentioned above. American Passages is actually a 16-part video course on American literature, accompanied by guides for students and instructors. The entire package, including the videos, is available from this site, on demand, over the Internet, at no cost—just fabulous!

# CHAPTER 4

# General Teacher Support

Teachers will return to the Web sites in this chapter again and again. Whether you seek supplemental activities for your textbook series, on-demand videos of exemplary teaching, the best lesson plans, technology tutorials, interactive learning experiences, best-of-the-Web guides, or the finest educational site on the Web, it's all here.

MarcoPolo is undoubtedly the best single educational resource on the Web. Besides an amazing array of original lesson plans and technology how-tos, it hosts excellent companion sites in the arts, humanities, economics, mathematics, language arts, science, and geography. Interdisciplinary, thematic, and discipline-specific lesson plans can be found at PBS TeacherSource, eThemes, The Educator's Reference Desk, Blue Web'n, and The WebQuest Page. Educational Web Adventures offers more than 75 interactive, in-depth, online learning experiences, some of which have won best in the world honors. AOL@SCHOOL contains plentiful resources for students and teachers. It's very strong on current events and science fairs, and provides a unique collection of extension activities in support of major textbook series in language arts, math, science, and social studies. Education World hosts a template library, technology tutorials, message boards, seven newsletters, research, lesson plans, rated Web links, and teacher tools. Annenberg/CPB Learner.org contains free, outstanding videos of exemplary teaching, 48 courses online, and scores of professional video workshops. Glencoe Online, from a major textbook publisher, overflows with lessons, enrichment materials, videos, maps, charts, and connections to off-site sources. It's nearly a whole high school on the Web.

# QUICK REFERENCE CHART

| General Teacher Support | FEATURES FOR TEACHERS | | | | | | |
|---|---|---|---|---|---|---|---|
| **Name of Site/URL** | chat or forum | lesson plans | teacher resources | parent resources | teacher's guide | video, audio, applets | Web links |
| **Annenberg/CPB Learner.org** www.learner.org | | | | | | | |
| **AOL@SCHOOL** www.aolatschool.com | | | | | | | |
| **Blue Web'n** www.kn.sbc.com/wired/bluewebn | | | | | | | |
| **Education World** www.educationworld.com | | | | | | | |
| **Educational Web Adventures (Eduweb)** www.eduweb.com | | | | | | | |
| **The Educator's Reference Desk** www.eduref.org | | | | | | | |
| **eThemes** www.emints.org/ethemes/ | | | | | | | |
| **Glencoe Online** www.glencoe.com/sec/ | | | | | | | |
| **MarcoPolo** www.marcopolo-education.org | | | | | | | |
| **PBS TeacherSource** www.pbs.org/teachersource/ | | | | | | | |
| **The WebQuest Page** webquest.sdsu.edu | | | | | | | |

The shaded boxes indicate the feature is available on the Web site.

# QUICK REFERENCE CHART *(continued)*

| General Teacher Support | FEATURES FOR TEACHERS | | | FEATURES FOR STUDENTS | | |
|---|---|---|---|---|---|---|
| Name of Site/URL | assessment ideas | e-newsletter | reproducibles | activities | interactive exercises | reading material |
| **Annenberg/CPB Learner.org** www.learner.org | | *Updates* | | | | |
| **AOL@SCHOOL** www.aolatschool.com | | | | | | |
| **Blue Web'n** www.kn.sbc.com/wired/bluewebn | | *Updates* | | | | |
| **Education World** www.educationworld.com | | numerous | | | | |
| **Educational Web Adventures (Eduweb)** www.eduweb.com | | | | | | |
| **The Educator's Reference Desk** www.eduref.org | | | | | | |
| **eThemes** www.emints.org/ethemes/ | | | | | | |
| **Glencoe Online** www.glencoe.com/sec/ | | *Teaching Today* | | | | |
| **MarcoPolo** www.marcopolo-education.org | | *MarcoGrams* | | | | |
| **PBS TeacherSource** www.pbs.org/teachersource/ | | *PBS Teacher Previews* | | | | |
| **The WebQuest Page** webquest.sdsu.edu | | | | | | |

The shaded boxes indicate the feature is available on the Web site.

## Annenberg/CPB Learner.org

**www.learner.org**

**SITE DESCRIPTION:** Learner.org is the first place to go for free professional development resources. It's an outstanding example of the power of the Internet to provide high-quality, on-demand services directly to the people who can benefit from them most. This site can trace its history back to 1981, when to improve education Walter Annenberg made a gift to the Corporation for Public Broadcasting. A second program in math and science began in 1990, and the two programs merged in 1999 to create Annenberg/CPB Learner.org.

Today, 48 separate courses and workshops are given on Annenberg/CPB, covering all major aspects of the K–12 curriculum. Each course or workshop is accompanied by extensive videos, support materials, activities, and a location to communicate with other participants. Annenberg/CPB provides certificates of participation which can be used for inservice or recertification credit. Graduate credit is available for courses and most workshops for a reasonable cost.

**HIGHLIGHTS FOR TEACHERS:** Videos are available directly on the Web for those with a high-speed connection. Videos may also be viewed on certain PBS stations or on a special satellite channel. All are available for purchase.

The various teaching-practices libraries offer numerous examples of real teachers in real classrooms doing great things. Take note of the **Learner.org for Students** button on the bottom left-hand side of the home page. This takes you to an area containing 11 interactive exhibits for students on such topics as **Volcanoes**, **Statistics**, **Math in Daily Life**, **Garbage**, and **Literature**. This area also provides eight more activity collections in math and science.

Courses and workshops are offered in arts, education theory and issues, history and social studies, literature and language arts, mathematics, and science. Some titles specifically for high school teachers include The Economics Classroom, Making Civics Real, Primary Sources, Teaching Geography, Artifacts & Fiction, Developing Writers, Teaching Math—Grades 9–12, Reactions in Chemistry, and Rediscovering Biology.

# AOL@SCHOOL

www.aolatschool.com

**SITE DESCRIPTION:** America Online (AOL) has put together a comprehensive and practical collection of materials for teachers. There's so much here, in fact, that it's helpful to take a few minutes to browse through the site before trying to use it for the first time. The Student Resources section is divided into **Primary**, **Elementary**, **Middle School**, and **High School** areas. Educator Resources has areas for **Teachers** and **Administrators**.

Under the four Student Resources areas, sections include **Subjects**, **Brainteasers**, **Study Kit**, **Research & Reference**, and **News and Current Events**. **High School** also provides a section on **College & Career**. The **Teachers** area is subdivided into **Subjects & Standards**, **Lesson Plans**, **Special Needs & Counseling**, **Professional Development**, **Classroom Tools & Tips**, **Education News**, and **Research & Reference**.

**HIGHLIGHTS FOR TEACHERS:** Since this site is maintained by AOL, teachers can be sure links have been carefully screened for content, appropriateness, and safety. There's a strong overall emphasis on current events, for both students and educators. This can be very convenient when you want to move back and forth between standard curriculum and what's happening in the news. Another helpful feature includes the unique **Textbook Activities** area, located within **Subjects & Standards** (under the **Teachers** link). Here, educators will find supplemental activities for all major textbooks, grouped by language arts, math, science, and social studies.

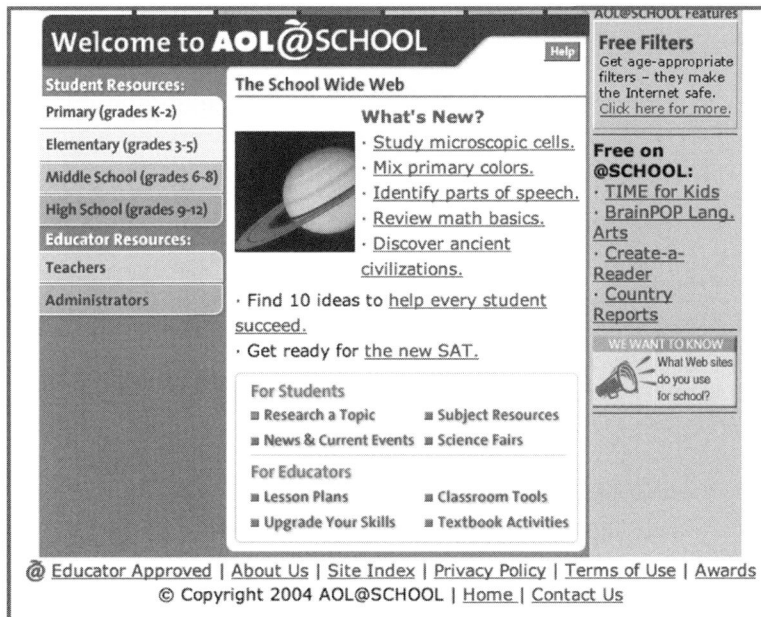

## Blue Web'n

**www.kn.sbc.com/wired/bluewebn**

**SITE DESCRIPTION:** When teachers are looking for a great Web site to spice up a unit, give students some background on a topic, start a project, or focus a specific lesson, Blue Web'n is a great place to start. It comprises more than 1,800 quality Web sites for learning, described and categorized by subject, grade level, and format.

The site is extremely well organized and user-friendly. Educators can search by grade level, subject area, or specific subcategories. The home page contains a fabulous matrix of 12 content areas (such as **Arts**, **English**, **History & Social Studies**, **Mathematics**, and **Science**) arranged into eight formats (Tools, References, Lesson Plans, Hotlists, Information Resources, Tutorials, Activities, and Projects). Five new sites are added each week, and users can sign up for a free e-mail newsletter.

**HIGHLIGHTS FOR TEACHERS:** Teachers can be sure that every site on Blue Web'n is a winner—the thousands of visitors every day make sure only the best are included. To find the best of the best, click on **Hot Site** in the bar above the matrix. This link takes you to annual lists of top resources going back to 1996. All sites are described thoroughly.

Blue Web'n also hosts Filamentality, "a fill-in-the-blank tool that guides you through picking a topic, searching the Web, gathering good Internet links, and turning them into learning links." This tool comes with a user-friendly tutorial and suggestions for use.

| Content Areas | Tools | References | Lesson Plans | Hotlists | Information Resources | Tutorials | Activities | Projects |
|---|---|---|---|---|---|---|---|---|
| Arts | 14 | 9 | 47 | 29 | 189 | 15 | 84 | 6 |
| Business | 1 | 2 | 10 | 8 | 39 | 5 | 17 | 1 |
| Community Interest | 47 | 74 | 33 | 40 | 284 | 16 | 91 | 10 |
| Education | 36 | 17 | 80 | 55 | 338 | 22 | 79 | 29 |
| English | 10 | 10 | 39 | 30 | 194 | 9 | 118 | 15 |
| Foreign Language | 3 | 7 | 9 | 11 | 48 | 5 | 24 | 1 |
| Health & Physical Education | 3 | 8 | 13 | 21 | 104 | 2 | 39 | 5 |
| History & Social Studies | 17 | 47 | 106 | 55 | 521 | 3 | 223 | 36 |
| Mathematics | 19 | 5 | 36 | 18 | 95 | 8 | 80 | 18 |
| Science | 15 | 31 | 120 | 39 | 432 | 22 | 234 | 68 |
| Technology (Applied Science) | 30 | 15 | 13 | 20 | 154 | 28 | 30 | 13 |
| Vocational Education | 1 | 8 | 18 | 5 | 77 | 9 | 35 | 2 |

## Education World

www.educationworld.com

**SITE DESCRIPTION:** Education World began in 1996 as a place to make using the Internet easier for K–12 educators. It contains original content for teachers and administrators, a search engine that focuses specifically on 500,000 education Web sites, employment listings, message boards, and links to seven free online newsletters covering many aspects of education, including education humor.

The home page offers useful material under the headings Lesson Planning, Professional Development, Administrator's Desk, Technology Integration, and School Issues. Special areas are devoted to financial planning, grants, and **Teacher Tools and Templates**.

**HIGHLIGHTS FOR TEACHERS:** A great place to start is the **"Best Of" Series**; you'll find a link to it near the bottom left-hand side of the home page, under Reference Center. Each year, Education World gathers the best of everything it's done and publishes a special summary. This collection, going back to 1997, is a gold mine of ideas and resources.

Two other areas not to be missed are the Technology in the Classroom Center (click on **Tech in Classroom**, on the left) and **Site Reviews**. The first includes a **Template Library** and dozens of **Techtorials** (step-by-step how-tos). They are extremely easy to follow and very practical. Education World also contains hundreds of teacher-submitted lesson plans and five-minute fillers.

# Educational Web Adventures

**www.eduweb.com**

**SITE DESCRIPTION:** Educational Web Adventures (Eduweb) is a company that designs online learning experiences. Since 1996, the company has produced more than 75 "immersive, interactive, and in-depth adventures about art, science and history." Most of the company's clients are museums and cultural institutions devoted to educating both students and the general public. A great many of Eduweb's projects have won "best of the Web" awards from prestigious international organizations.

This Web site gives access to all of Eduweb's adventures. They're organized in several different ways, including by subject, grade, most current, and client. Each adventure is well described, and the awards it has won are noted. All the sites are highly interactive and educational. Many contain lesson plans as well.

**HIGHLIGHTS FOR TEACHERS:** Some of the sites for high school students that have garnered the highest awards include **World Myths & Legends**, **ArtEventures**, **Understanding Slavery**, and **Amazon Interactive**. For a lot of fun, check out the **Soul Learning** site, created for the Stax Museum of American Soul Music.

## The Educator's Reference Desk

www.eduref.org

**SITE DESCRIPTION:** Here's where educators can find the resources formerly housed at AskERIC. When the U.S. Department of Education ceased to support the ERIC system in late 2003, many of the ERIC Clearinghouses migrated to new settings; AskERIC was one of the most popular, and Educator's Reference Desk maintains many of its best features.

Educator's Reference Desk contains four tabs: **Resource Guides**, **Lesson Plans**, **Question Archives**, and **Search GEM/ERIC** (a search function for the ERIC database). The **Resource Guides** tab includes collections of Web sites in 16 **Subjects** such as arts, character education, integrated interdisciplinary approach, language arts, math, science, and social studies. The **Lesson Plans** tab gathers more than 2,000 teacher-written and quality-checked lesson plans in 13 subject areas. The **Question Archives** catalog gives responses to selected questions asked between 1992 and 2003 (questions are no longer being accepted).

**HIGHLIGHTS FOR TEACHERS:** For most teachers, **Resource Guides** and **Lesson Plans** will be the most consistently useful sections. For example, go to **Resource Guides**, then **Subjects** to find hundreds of links to sites in 16 curriclum areas. Go to **Resource Guides**, then **General Education**, then **Learning Theories** to find a list of 20 resources.

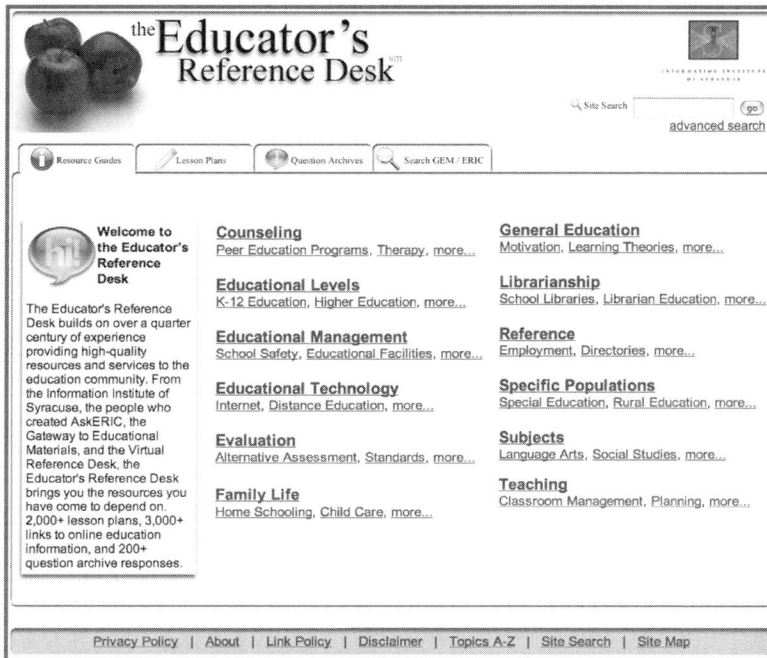

## eThemes

**www.emints.org/ethemes/**

**SITE DESCRIPTION:** This database collects Web sites and organizes them around specific themes. Graduate students assess the quality of the sites, grade-level appropriateness, and connection to state standards. They also write a short description of each. More than 750 themes have been identified so far, with more added every week.

Go to **Resource Index** to browse eThemes alphabetically or by grade level. You can also search the site by specifying grade level and one or more keywords. Click on **Newest eThemes** at the top of the home page to see the collections added within the past two weeks.

**HIGHLIGHTS FOR TEACHERS:** The **eThemes Calendar**, located at the top of the home page, offers great help for those moments when you need something constructive to fill up unexpected free time.

For each day of the month, eThemes has selected an activity-based educational site that students can use with a minimum of supervision.

Descriptions of individual sites are well written and enable teachers to quickly select sites they wish to use. Searching the database is very easy on this site, and because no graphics are used, pages load quickly.

## Glencoe Online

www.glencoe.com/sec/

**SITE DESCRIPTION:** Textbook publishers have become increasingly driven to place resources online; some have even begun to bring out online textbooks. Glencoe, one of the premier publishers of secondary texts, has chosen to place an abundance of materials online to supplement its books. Since Glencoe (a division of McGraw-Hill) maintains an extensive catalog of text series and individual books, this Web site serves as a gold mine for nearly all secondary educators.

The site lists 21 separate curricular areas, including **Art**, **Music**, **Driver Education**, **Mathematics**, **Science**, **Social Studies**, **Literature**, **Language Arts**, **World Languages**, **Health & Fitness**, **Computer Education**, and **Business Administration**. Each curricular area provides supplementary materials keyed directly to standards-based texts. The resources vary from subject to subject and may include student activities beyond the textbook. These activities include videos, teacher lesson plans, suggested student projects, self-scoring personality inventories, maps, charts, diagrams, connections to off-site materials such as *Time* magazine, Web links, WebQuests, interactive tutorials, flashcards, vocabulary exercises, self-check quizzes, and interdisciplinary connections.

**HIGHLIGHTS FOR TEACHERS:** Glencoe Online has plentiful materials for both students and teachers, and even some articles and tips for parents.

A great place to begin is **Teaching Today**, an online magazine for high school and middle school teachers. Along with a **New Teacher Survival Guide** (click on the icon on the right), it contains a teaching tip of the day, subject-specific resources, Web-based resources, specific aids for middle school educators, and an ever-growing collection of downloadable materials (graphic organizers, student activities, classroom management tips, test-prep ideas, and technology integration tips). The writers at **Teaching Today** have done a terrific job of identifying links to recommended sites for research, deeper study, and enrichment. The Subject-Specific Resources category contains articles directed toward the needs of English language learners, differentiating instruction, testing, and technology integration.

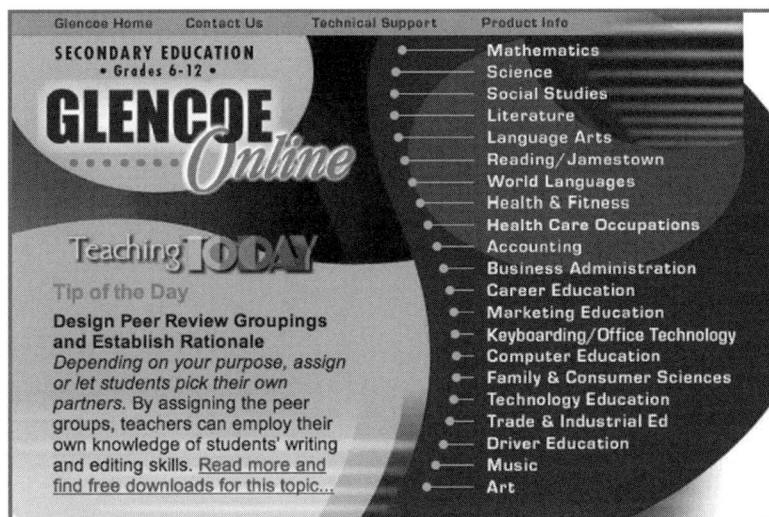

## MarcoPolo

**www.marcopolo-education.org**

**SITE DESCRIPTION:** MarcoPolo is the best educational Web site online today. Of course, like many great sites, it's really a collection of a number of sites that also exist independently. The partner sites linked from the home page are all exceptional in their own right and contain oceans of original content and resources for K–12. Material unique to MarcoPolo includes **Teacher Resources**, where you can find information on standards alignment, how to use MarcoPolo, the MarcoPolo calendar, free access to the monthly MarcoGram newsletter and the MarcoPolo e-mail list, and a download link to a free PDF copy of the *Secondary Teacher's Guide*. In **Professional Development**, you can access online courses, identify live instructor-led MarcoPolo courses in your area, and download teacher training resources.

**HIGHLIGHTS FOR TEACHERS:** Here are just a few features you'll find on the partner sites:

- **ARTSEDGE:** Arts education from the Kennedy Center in Washington, D.C. Search nearly 300 lessons by subject and discipline to prepare interdisciplinary activities.

- **EconEdLink/CyberTeach:** From the National Council on Economics Education. Click on **Lessons**, sort by grade, and find more than 100 lessons and activities.

- **EDSITEment:** Art and culture, literature and language arts, foreign language, and history and social studies from the National Endowment for the Humanities. Click on **Calendar** for a monthly calendar that features activities for just about every day of the month.

- **Illuminations:** From the National Council of Teachers of Mathematics. Click on **Tools** to locate 15 math activities you can use to explore math and create interactive lessons.

- **ReadWriteThink:** From the International Reading Association and the National Council of Teachers of English. Click on **Student Materials** for more than 30 interactive literacy tools linked to specific lessons.

- **Xpeditions:** From the National Geographic Society. **Atlas** provides free, downloadable maps for nearly every part of the world.

## PBS TeacherSource

www.pbs.org/teachersource/

**SITE DESCRIPTION:** The Public Broadcasting Service (PBS) Web site for teachers is clearly organized and laid out without a lot of jumble; it's a breeze to find what you're looking for. Browse through a collection of 4,500 lesson plans and activities divided into sections titled **Arts & Literature**, **Health & Fitness**, **Math**, **Science**, **Social Studies**, **Pre K–2**, and **Library Media**. Many resources are based on programs broadcast on PBS stations; most are keyed to state standards and provide extensive information and recommendations for in-depth study options.

Through a grant from the U.S. Department of Education, PBS TeacherSource offers both technology integration and extensive online professional development in core curriculum areas. The site also has a special Math Academy program for K–12 teachers in collaboration with the National Council of Teachers of Mathematics. In addition, it provides tutorials on common uses of technology in the classroom.

**HIGHLIGHTS FOR TEACHERS:** Above and beyond its excellent collection of lesson plans, PBS TeacherSource publishes **Concepts Across the Curriculum**, a series of interdisciplinary units for students in Grades 3–12 on such topics as diversity and achievement, culture and history, the arts, science and health, and family and community. Teachers should also look at **Current Events for the Classroom**, from NewsHour, a separate collection of outstanding resources.

Educators may personalize PBS TeacherSource so that it shows only information related to the topics and grade levels you prefer. You can also navigate through **Get Local** to access outreach from your local PBS station, check taping rights for shows, look at broadcast schedules, and receive an e-mail newsletter.

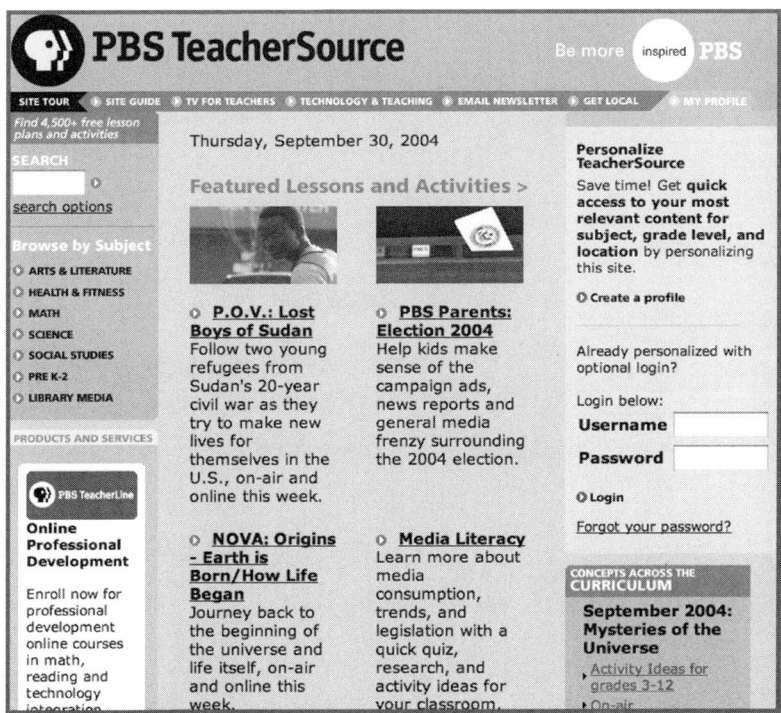

## The WebQuest Page

**webquest.sdsu.edu**

**SITE DESCRIPTION:** A WebQuest (for those who may be wondering) is described on this site as "an inquiry-oriented activity in which most or all of the information used by learners is drawn from the Web. WebQuests are designed to use learners' time well, to focus on using information rather than looking for it, and to support learners' thinking at the levels of analysis, synthesis, and evaluation." WebQuests are one of the best and most original contributions to education that computers and the Internet have made possible.

This site is maintained by Bernie Dodge, one of the originators (along with Tom March) of the WebQuest concept. Most educators will find the areas of greatest interest to be **Overview & FAQ**, which orients you to the WebQuest concept and the site; **Training Materials**, which provides access to more than 30 WebQuest articles and training materials; and **Portal**, which hosts a forum bulletin board and a superb collection of sample WebQuests.

**HIGHLIGHTS FOR TEACHERS:** Teachers should definitely click on **Portal** and spend some time browsing through the **Top** WebQuests. As of this writing, more than 600 have been evaluated and given top ranking. They are conveniently displayed in a matrix by grade level (K–2, 3–5, 6–8, 9–12, and Adult) and by subject matter. Subjects include Art & Music, Business, English/Language Arts, Foreign Language, Health/PE, Life Skills/Careers, Math, Social Studies, Science, Professional Skills, and Technology.

For a quick introduction to the concept, visit the section A WebQuest about WebQuests. The link is in the right-hand column on the **Training Materials** page.

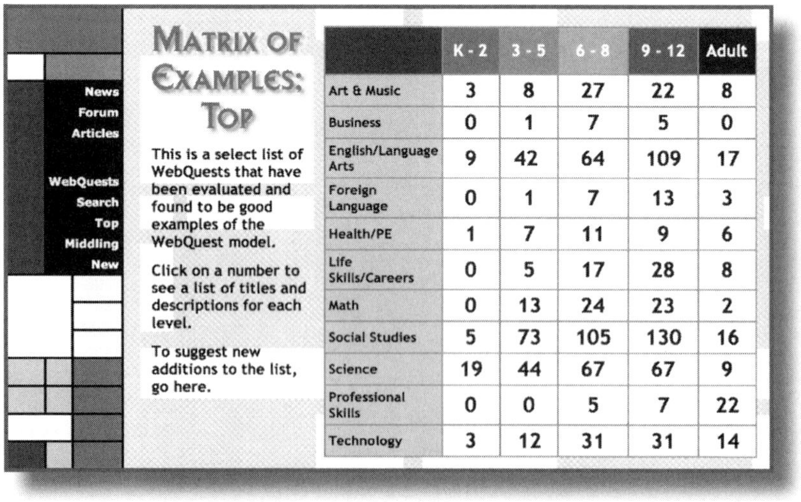

### MATRIX OF EXAMPLES: TOP

This is a select list of WebQuests that have been evaluated and found to be good examples of the WebQuest model.

Click on a number to see a list of titles and descriptions for each level.

To suggest new additions to the list, go here.

| | K - 2 | 3 - 5 | 6 - 8 | 9 - 12 | Adult |
|---|---|---|---|---|---|
| Art & Music | 3 | 8 | 27 | 22 | 8 |
| Business | 0 | 1 | 7 | 5 | 0 |
| English/Language Arts | 9 | 42 | 64 | 109 | 17 |
| Foreign Language | 0 | 1 | 7 | 13 | 3 |
| Health/PE | 1 | 7 | 11 | 9 | 6 |
| Life Skills/Careers | 0 | 5 | 17 | 28 | 8 |
| Math | 0 | 13 | 24 | 23 | 2 |
| Social Studies | 5 | 73 | 105 | 130 | 16 |
| Science | 19 | 44 | 67 | 67 | 9 |
| Professional Skills | 0 | 0 | 5 | 7 | 22 |
| Technology | 3 | 12 | 31 | 31 | 14 |

Sidebar navigation: News, Forum, Articles, WebQuests, Search, Top, Middling, New

# CHAPTER 5

# Health and PE

This chapter includes Web sites with a fabulous assortment of materials and ideas for health and physical education teachers. Teachers will find lesson plans, activities, and ideas for physical education at PE Central and PELINKS4U. Materials devoted to teen health issues are available at TeensHealth and Wired for Health. Nutrition Navigator, from Tufts University, reviews and rates nutrition Web sites. At The Reconstructors Solve Medical Mysteries site, there's an interactive game (complete with an extensive teacher's guide) that challenges students to solve whodunits about infectious diseases.

# QUICK REFERENCE CHART

| Health and PE | FEATURES FOR TEACHERS | | | | | | |
|---|---|---|---|---|---|---|---|
| Name of Site/URL | chat or forum | lesson plans | teacher resources | parent resources | teacher's guide | video, audio, applets | Web links |
| **Nutrition Navigator: A Rating Guide to Nutrition Web Sites** navigator.tufts.edu | | | ▓ | | | | ▓ |
| **PE Central** www.pecentral.org | | ▓ | ▓ | | | | |
| **PELINKS4U** www.pelinks4u.org | ▓ | ▓ | ▓ | | | | ▓ |
| **The Reconstructors Solve Medical Mysteries** medmyst.rice.edu | | ▓ | | | ▓ | ▓ | |
| **TeensHealth** www.kidshealth.org/teen/ | | | | ▓ | | | |
| **Wired for Health** www.wiredforhealth.gov.uk | | ▓ | ▓ | ▓ | ▓ | | ▓ |

The shaded boxes indicate the feature is available on the Web site.

## QUICK REFERENCE CHART *(continued)*

| Health and PE | FEATURES FOR TEACHERS | | | FEATURES FOR STUDENTS | | |
|---|---|---|---|---|---|---|
| **Name of Site/URL** | assessment ideas | e-newsletter | reproducibles | activities | interactive exercises | reading material |
| **Nutrition Navigator: A Rating Guide to Nutrition Web Sites** navigator.tufts.edu | | | | | | ▓ |
| **PE Central** www.pecentral.org | ▓ | *PE Central Newsletter* | | ▓ | ▓ | ▓ |
| **PELINKS4U** www.pelinks4u.org | ▓ | *PE News* | | ▓ | ▓ | ▓ |
| **The Reconstructors Solve Medical Mysteries** medmyst.rice.edu | ▓ | | | ▓ | ▓ | ▓ |
| **TeensHealth** www.kidshealth.org/teen/ | | | | ▓ | ▓ | ▓ |
| **Wired for Health** www.wiredforhealth.gov.uk | ▓ | | | ▓ | ▓ | ▓ |

The shaded boxes indicate the feature is available on the Web site.

## Nutrition Navigator: A Rating Guide to Nutrition Web Sites
navigator.tufts.edu

**SITE DESCRIPTION:** Nutrition Navigator gets right to the point. Developers claim it's "the first online rating and review guide that solves the two major problems Web users have when seeking nutrition information: how to quickly find information best suited to their needs and whether to trust the information they find." Online nutrition sites are rated four times each year by a team from Tufts University.

Sites are evaluated on nutrition accuracy, depth of nutrition information, how recently the site was updated, and user friendliness. Each site receives a numerical rating from 1 to 25 and is described in a brief paragraph. Site reviews are grouped into the following categories: **Women, Men, Family, Seniors, General Nutrition, Health Professionals, Educators, Journalists, Weight Management,** and **Special Dietary Needs.** Within each category, rated sites are placed into groups: Among the Best, Better than Most, Average, and Not Recommended. Nutrition Navigator accepts no advertising.

**HIGHLIGHTS FOR TEACHERS:** In the **Educators** area, 19 Web sites are rated as Among the Best. Interestingly, as of this writing, the top-rated site—Dole 5-A-Day—is sponsored by Dole Food Company. Many of the sites contain educational resources for use with students, including Dole 5-A-Day, Children with Diabetes, Dairy Council of California, Feeding Minds and Fighting Hunger, and Fight BAC.

# PE Central

## www.pecentral.org

**SITE DESCRIPTION:** PE Central houses the Web's most comprehensive resources for health and PE educators. Originally founded by graduate students at Virginia Tech, this spot now boasts more than 100 editors and advisers from across the United States and around the world. The site is organized into 19 topical sections, including lesson plans, assessment ideas, instructional resources, links to health and PE Web sites, fitness logs, products, and comprehensive school-wide programs.

PE Central also publishes a free e-mail newsletter of articles, news, and product information. It's sent monthly to more than 18,000 subscribers. The site is searchable and user-friendly.

**HIGHLIGHTS FOR TEACHERS:** Don't miss the **Best Practices Program**, listing well over 100 creative ideas. **Instructional Resources** offers nearly 50 outstanding programs as well as other aids, all available on the Web. The **Adapted Physical Education** area is another valuable resource, with 16 subsections of its own.

PE Central's most powerful element is its outstanding and easy-to-use collection of 1,800 lesson plans and ideas. Click on **Lesson Ideas** on the home page and you're taken to a page with 16 links to an excellent and growing collection of ideas to help you make health and physical education classes a time of enjoyable and productive learning for all.

## PELINKS4U

**www.pelinks4u.org**

**SITE DESCRIPTION:** PELINKS4U is the *New York Times* of the physical education field: comprehensive and skillful, it takes a distinctly intellectual approach to what it covers. PELINKS4U is developed and maintained by a group of teachers and researchers at Central Washington University.

It's difficult to imagine any aspect of health and physical education this site hasn't covered. Like a newspaper, it has different sections, tabbed at the top of the home page: **Adapted PE**; **Coaching & Sports**; **Elementary PE**; **Health, Fitness & Nutrition**; **Interdisciplinary PE**; **Secondary PE**; and **Technology in PE**. Book reviews are also included, as well as a store, a calendar for national conferences and workshops, and a forum for discussion. Readers can also subscribe to an e-mail newsletter.

**HIGHLIGHTS FOR TEACHERS:** PELINKS4U began publication in 1999, and all issues are contained in an archive, accessible from the drop-down menu at the top left side of every page. Apparently, its publication schedule has varied from weekly to monthly; right now it seems to be on a monthly schedule, with perhaps one issue during the summer.

As a result of its newsmagazine-like structure, the site provides great news and updates. If you want to dig deeply into a topic or find a collection of resources on a particular subject, the **Search** function works quite well.

## The Reconstructors Solve Medical Mysteries

**medmyst.rice.edu**

**SITE DESCRIPTION:** This interactive game, MedMyst for short, is set in the future. Players are called on to solve medical mysteries involving infectious diseases. The game has three adventures, one focused on infectious diseases in general, the second on cholera, and the third on poxes. Each has its own learning objectives. Players take on the roles of scientist, historian, and detective. The game action should engage most middle school and lower-grade high school students (and probably a teacher or two, as well).

**HIGHLIGHTS FOR TEACHERS:** This is no mere game site; the educational content is significant, and teacher support is plentiful. Click on **Teacher Pages** in the upper left-hand corner to find links for **Learning Objectives, Teaching Materials,** and pre- and post-**Testing Materials. Teaching Materials** is intended for use both before and after playing the game. Click on **Cool Links** and you'll be taken to lists of sites connected to the central subject for each adventure. There's also the **MedMyst Magazine,** which can be printed out for student reference.

MedMyst has gained recognition from numerous prestigious organizations, such as the American Association for the Advancement of Science and the *Washington Times.* It's produced by Rice University's Center for Technology in Teaching and Learning.

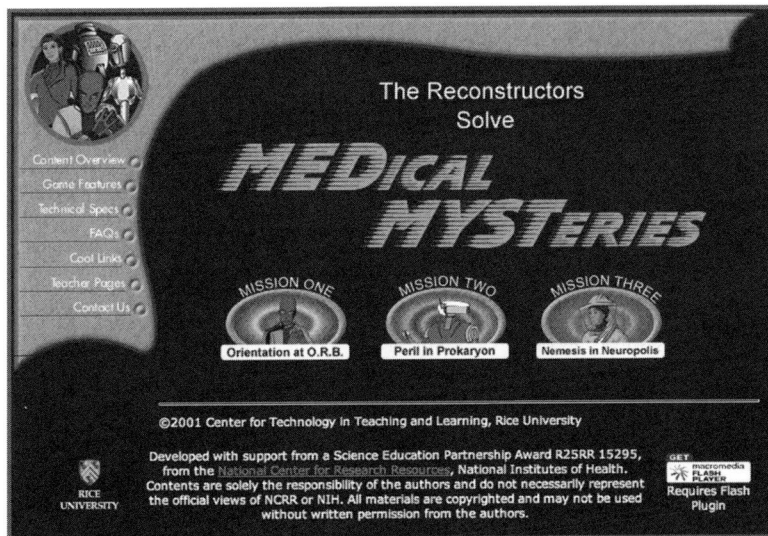

## TeensHealth

**www.kidshealth.org/teen/**

**SITE DESCRIPTION:** This site is part of the larger KidsHealth Web site supported by the Nemours Foundation. It's one of the oldest and most trusted spots on the Internet for reliable health information and has garnered numerous prestigious awards.

TeensHealth consists of 12 sections that contain "honest, accurate information about health, relationships, and growing up." Topics addressed include **Your Body**, **Your Mind**, **Sexual Health**, **Food & Fitness**, **Recipes**, **Drugs & Alcohol**, **Diseases & Conditions**, **Infections**, **School & Jobs**, and **Staying Safe**. There's also a collection of articles in Spanish.

**HIGHLIGHTS FOR TEACHERS:** TeensHealth gives straight talk to young people and doesn't speak down to them. Each section provides informative articles that are clearly indexed to make them easy to find. It's a great place for teenagers to research health-related topics, and they can visit the site to locate information they might be embarrassed to ask someone about. The recipes for students with diabetes, cystic fibrosis, celiac disease, or lactose intolerance (as well as the recipes for vegetarians) are fascinating, and they sound delicious.

## Wired for Health

www.wiredforhealth.gov.uk

**SITE DESCRIPTION:** This Web site was established by several departments of the national government in Great Britain to provide accurate and engaging information related to the health and well-being of children and young people. Wired for Health is divided into four main sections: **Teachers**, **Local Healthy Schools Programme Coordinators** (this site is from the United Kingdom, after all), **Education and Health Professionals**, and **Young People**. Four separate areas based on age are provided for young people: **Welltown** (ages 5–7), **Galaxy-H** (ages 7–11), **LifeBytes** (ages 11–14), and **Mind, Body, and Soul** (ages 14–16). Each of these contains information, games, and other interactive features. Topics are addressed on an age-appropriate basis, and the sites are attractive and interesting. Topics include alcohol use, drugs, emotional health and well-being, healthy eating, physical activity, safety, sex and relationships, smoking, and pupil health.

**HIGHLIGHTS FOR TEACHERS:** Each of the four student Web areas contains extensive support for teachers, including lesson plans and teaching guides for every activity. In addition, the **Teachers** area contains numerous **Case Studies** of best practices in health education, guidance on how to motivate students to participate in health education, and links to further resources for professional development. The **Site Map** provides a very helpful guide to navigating through the entire site.

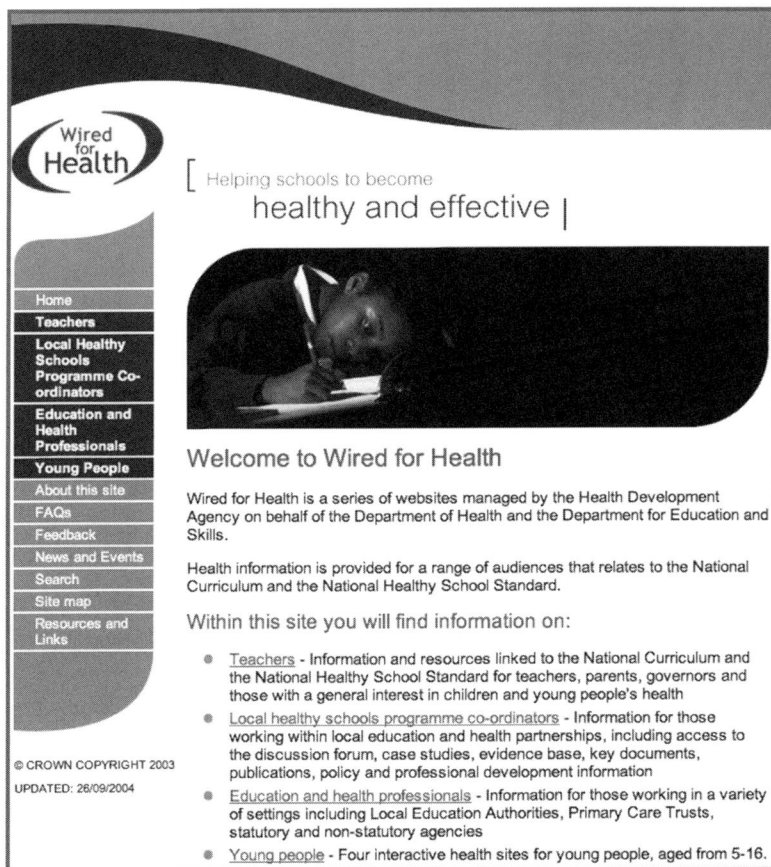

# CHAPTER 6

# Mathematics

**A**dd up the tremendous resources available on the Web sites in this chapter and you'll be well on your way to transforming your mathematics curriculum. Applets and other multimedia applications found here excel in illustrating and clarifying important mathematical concepts and functions. Hundreds of these interactives can be found at E-Examples, Fun Mathematics Lessons, Illuminations (see MarcoPolo in chapter 4), Mathematics Materials for Tomorrow's Teachers, the National Library of Virtual Manipulatives, Shodor Education Foundation, and Culturally Situated Design Tools. The latter connects African, African American, Native American, and Latino cultures with beginning-to-advanced topics in geometry, symmetry, modular math, pre-algebra, and fractions.

Teachers will find numerous lesson and unit plans at the Eisenhower National Clearinghouse and The Math Forum, along with ask-an-expert services, enrichment activities, and further online teaching tools. Problem sets designed to offer clear connections to real-world situations are located at Learning Wave Communications: Engage Your Brain, Fun Mathematics Lessons, and Problems with a Point. Middle school teachers in particular will want to explore the extremely detailed and comprehensive teacher guides at Mathematics Materials for Tomorrow's Teachers. Figure This! Math Challenges for Families contains at least two years' worth of activities to engage middle school students and their families. Finally, the Center for Technology and Teacher Education shines in its math offerings, and Tools for Understanding makes use of spreadsheets and calculators to teach math creatively.

# QUICK REFERENCE CHART

| Mathematics | FEATURES FOR TEACHERS | | | | | | |
|---|---|---|---|---|---|---|---|
| Name of Site/URL | chat or forum | lesson plans | teacher resources | parent resources | teacher's guide | video, audio, applets | Web links |
| **Center for Technology and Teacher Education: Mathematics** www.teacherlink.org/content/math/ | | | | | | | |
| **Culturally Situated Design Tools: Teaching Math Through Culture** www.rpi.edu/~eglash/csdt.html | | | | | | | |
| **E-Examples** standards.nctm.org/document/ eexamples/ | | | | | | | |
| **Eisenhower National Clearing-house for Mathematics and Science Education (ENC)** www.enc.org | | | | | | | |
| **Figure This! Math Challenges for Families** www.figurethis.org | | | | | | | |
| **Fun Mathematics Lessons by Cynthia Lanius** math.rice.edu/~lanius/Lessons/ | | | | | | | |
| **Learning Wave Communica-tions: Engage Your Brain** www.learningwave.com/menu.html | | | | | | | |
| **Math Forum@Drexel** mathforum.org | | | | | | | |
| **Mathematics Materials for Tomorrow's Teachers** www.mste.uiuc.edu/m2t2/ | | | | | | | |
| **National Library of Virtual Manipulatives for Interactive Mathematics** matti.usu.edu/nlvm/nav/ | | | | | | | |
| **Problems with a Point** www2.edc.org/mathproblems/ | | | | | | | |
| **Shodor Education Foundation** www.shodor.org | | | | | | | |
| **Tools for Understanding** www.ups.edu/community/tofu/ | | | | | | | |

The shaded boxes indicate the feature is available on the Web site.

# QUICK REFERENCE CHART *(continued)*

| Mathematics | FEATURES FOR TEACHERS | | | FEATURES FOR STUDENTS | | |
|---|---|---|---|---|---|---|
| **Name of Site/URL** | assessment ideas | e-newsletter | reproducibles | activities | interactive exercises | reading material |
| **Center for Technology and Teacher Education: Mathematics** www.teacherlink.org/content/math/ | | | | | | |
| **Culturally Situated Design Tools: Teaching Math Through Culture** www.rpi.edu/~eglash/csdt.html | | | | | | |
| **E-Examples** standards.nctm.org/document/ eexamples/ | | | | | | |
| **Eisenhower National Clearinghouse for Mathematics and Science Education (ENC)** www.enc.org | | *ENC Updates* | | | | |
| **Figure This! Math Challenges for Families** www.figurethis.org | | | | | | |
| **Fun Mathematics Lessons by Cynthia Lanius** math.rice.edu/~lanius/Lessons/ | | | | | | |
| **Learning Wave Communications: Engage Your Brain** www.learningwave.com/menu.html | | | | | | |
| **Math Forum@Drexel** mathforum.org | | *Math Forum Internet News* | | | | |
| **Mathematics Materials for Tomorrow's Teachers** www.mste.uiuc.edu/m2t2/ | | | | | | |
| **National Library of Virtual Manipulatives for Interactive Mathematics** matti.usu.edu/nlvm/nav/ | | | | | | |
| **Problems with a Point** www2.edc.org/mathproblems/ | | | | | | |
| **Shodor Education Foundation** www.shodor.org | | | | | | |
| **Tools for Understanding** www.ups.edu/community/tofu/ | | | | | | |

The shaded boxes indicate the feature is available on the Web site.

## Center for Technology and Teacher Education: Mathematics
www.teacherlink.org/content/math/

**SITE DESCRIPTION:** The Center for Technology and Teacher Education at the University of Virginia produces this site. Resources are provided to support the teaching of English, mathematics, science, and social studies. The mathematics area is the most robust and instructive.

The areas of the site of most immediate interest to secondary teachers will be **Project Activities** (activities for the use of graphing calculators, The Geometer's Sketchpad, Excel, the ExploreMath.com Web site, Global Positioning Systems, and MicroWorlds Logo), **Interactive Projects** (addressing fractals, probability, normal distribution, projectile motion, and geometry), and **Related Links**.

**HIGHLIGHTS FOR TEACHERS:** The selection and use of software programs in the **Project Activities** area signifies, among other things, that these tools have become the standards for teaching mathematics. **Interactive Projects** contains a variety of exercises involving spreadsheets, flash animation, the Sierpinski Polygon, lessons in geometry, and probability.

The **Related Links** section is especially useful because the lists are selective and relatively short. Each entry is well described. The four areas covered include: **Geometry and the Geometer's Sketchpad**, **Interactive Mathematics Web Sites**, **Mathematics and History of Mathematics**, and **Useful Web Sites for Collecting Data**.

## Culturally Situated Design Tools: Teaching Math Through Culture
**www.rpi.edu/~eglash/csdt.html**

**SITE DESCRIPTION:** This Web site offers 10 well-designed applets based on themes representing Africa, African Americans, the youth subculture, Native Americans, and Latinos. The applets address topics in fractal geometry, transformational geometry, Cartesian and polar coordinates, modular math, symmetry, pre-algebra, and fractions. Students learn these concepts by viewing and interacting with a wide variety of cultural artifacts, including Native American beadwork, African sculpture, ancient Mayan temples, graffiti, and Latin percussion rhythms.

The site is simply laid out, with a minimum of graphics. The design tools easily lend themselves to standards-based curricula and are very intuitive. This is an exciting and eye-opening site for students and teachers alike.

**HIGHLIGHTS FOR TEACHERS:** The Web site is divided into five areas based on ethnic category. Each area contains a cultural background section, a tutorial, the applet itself, and a teaching materials section that includes lesson plans, evaluation instruments, samples of student work, and other support.

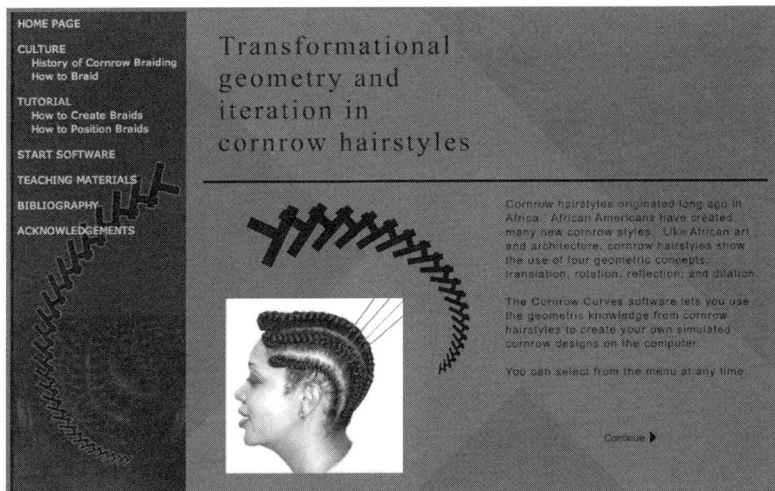

## E-Examples

**standards.nctm.org/document/eexamples/**

**SITE DESCRIPTION:** This stunning Web site consists of a powerful collection of 22 interactive activities developed by the National Council of Teachers of Mathematics (NCTM) as part of its larger Web project called Principles and Standards for School Mathematics. The electronic examples are designed to actualize the principles that underlie the NCTM standards by adding interactivity, motion, and graphics. The site's organization parallels the four grade bands used by NCTM in its well-known standards: PK–2, 3–5, 6–8, and 9–12.

Most of the activities consist of multiple parts, with additional tasks for students, discussion for teachers, and thought-provoking questions for reflection. Ample support for the teacher is provided in text material that can be accessed through links at the top of each activity page.

**HIGHLIGHTS FOR TEACHERS:** Each activity takes a significant concept and brings it to life. Examples include **Creating, Describing, and Analyzing Patterns** to Recognize Relationships and Make Predictions; **Learning About Number Relationships** and Properties of Numbers Using Calculators and Hundred Boards; **Understanding Distance, Speed, and Time** Relationships Using Simulation Software; **Collecting, Representing, and Interpreting Data** Using Spreadsheets and Graphic Software; and **Learning about Length, Perimeter, Area, and Volume** of Similar Objects Using Interactive Figures.

[How to Use the Interactive Figure]

Rubber Band

Delete Node
Delete Band
Clear All

[Stand-alone applet]

### Talking about Triangles in the Classroom

Students enjoy working with geoboards, whether they are interactive computer geoboards or physical ones. As with any manipulative, students need ample time to explore the material before specific tasks are presented.

# Eisenhower National Clearinghouse for Mathematics and Science Education

**www.enc.org**

**SITE DESCRIPTION:** The Eisenhower National Clearinghouse (ENC) Web site is an extraordinarily comprehensive and valuable resource. Although intended primarily as a teacher resource center in mathematics and science, it has features useful for educators in virtually all content areas. The site is organized into five outstanding sections: **Classroom Calendar**, which contains background information, activities, and curriculum materials dealing with biographies, inventions, reading lists, math, and science; **Digital Dozen**, a monthly collection of exemplary math and science Web sites for teachers and students; **ENC Focus**, an online magazine dealing with math and science for teachers; a rich collection of **Lessons & Activities**; and **Ask ENC**, a service through which anyone over 18 may seek free assistance from ENC reference librarians regarding information, materials, and Web sites.

Additional features include **Web Links**, **Curriculum Resources**, **Education Topics** (articles on subjects such as interdisciplinary strategies, technology, inquiry and problem solving, innovative curriculum materials, and real-world math and science), and **Professional Development** support services.

**HIGHLIGHTS FOR TEACHERS:** Of ENC's numerous great features, one of the best is the **By Your Own Design** individual professional development program, co-created by ENC and the National Staff Development Council. This free online resource enables teachers, staff developers, and principals to design and participate in a personalized learning plan, complete with self-assessment tools.

For those interested in news about education nationwide, ENC publishes a daily set of links to education-related stories from newspapers, magazines and online journals. All of ENC's resources are well organized, of high quality, and very convenient to search.

## Figure This! Math Challenges for Families

**www.figurethis.org**

**SITE DESCRIPTION:** Figure This! is a wonderful place for middle school students and their families. The site is designed to get students and parents working together on a series of engaging math exercises. It's the perfect foundation on which to build a parent-involvement program and improve students' math achievement at the same time. The materials are presented in both Spanish and English, and an introductory video and a PowerPoint presentation are included. The site has been developed by the National Council of Teachers of Mathematics (NCTM) through grants from the National Science Foundation and the U.S. Department of Education.

Figure This! addresses all of the major areas of the NCTM standards for middle school math: algebra, geometry, measurement, number, and statistics and probability. The complete program has 80 intriguing problems. A full solution is provided for each, along with a description of the math involved and its usefulness in the real world. The challenges feature tips for getting started, fun facts, ideas for further exploration, and additional problems and solutions.

**HIGHLIGHTS FOR TEACHERS:** The math challenges are designed to be done outside of school in family settings. Special materials are included so that teachers or coordinators can make presentations to families, answer frequently asked questions, and address adults' reluctance to get involved. A separate section, **Family Corner**, is included on the Web site for exactly this purpose. Middle schoolers and their families have a sufficient number of challenges and extension activities to keep them busy for two or more years.

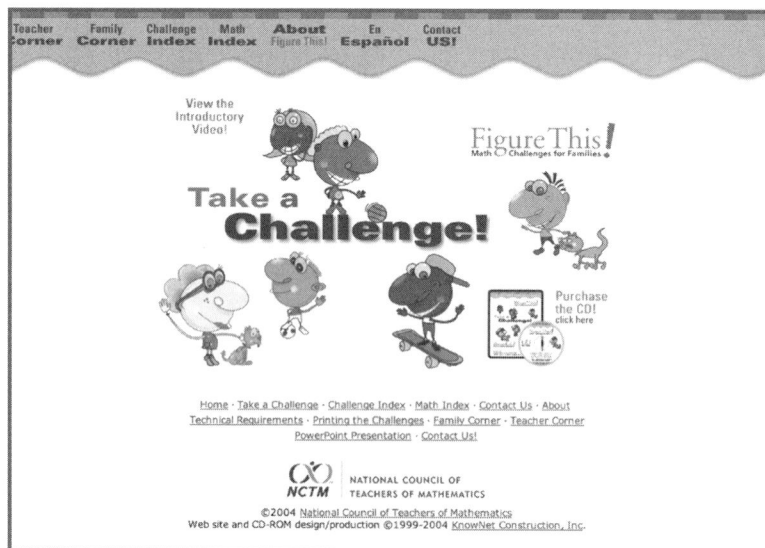

## Fun Mathematics Lessons by Cynthia Lanius

**math.rice.edu/~lanius/Lessons/**

**SITE DESCRIPTION:** This is another site that demonstrates how one dedicated and very talented individual can create a top-notch Web site. Cynthia Lanius has gathered a wonderful collection of math activities for students from kindergarten to college age. All lessons and activities are keyed to national and Texas state mathematics standards. Links are provided to additional Web sites that explore the same topics, and many of the sections offer extensive support for teachers. Activities are designed to be printed out or completed on the computer; a number of them are in Spanish as well as English.

**HIGHLIGHTS FOR TEACHERS:** The activities on this site can be powerful motivators and lesson extenders; they can enliven lessons as well as illustrate concepts. Use them with a projector or a SmartBoard for a great change of pace.

Scroll to the bottom of the home page to see a description of all the available lessons. By rolling your cursor over the name of the lesson, the display tells you the math topic (counting, algebra, fractions, graphing, problem solving, geometry, etc.) and grade level, and it provides a capsulized write-up of the concepts and procedures covered in the lesson. Highlights include **Geometry Online**, **Fun and Sun Rent-a-Car**, and the very thoughtful questions in **The Hot Tub**.

**Visualizing An Infinite Series**

Consider the yellow trapezoids in the series below:

$1/4$

$+ (1/4)^2$

$+ (1/4)^3$

$+ \ldots + (1/4)^n + \ldots = ?$

[To the Top] [Next] [More Fun Mathematics ]

## Learning Wave Communications: Engage Your Brain
**www.learningwave.com/menu.html**

**SITE DESCRIPTION:** This Web site offers a healthy selection of math activities for students in middle school and early high school. Each activity is designed in a visually and intellectually appealing format. Most will require close reading and several steps to find the answer.

The activities are excellent preparation for standardized and state assessment tests. Working through this site is analogous to weight training for athletes: the activities are at least as difficult and complex as those on the high-stakes tests, if not more so. Students build their test-taking muscles and learn strategies that will help them on test day.

**HIGHLIGHTS FOR TEACHERS:** On the Engage Your Brain home page, you'll find four activity collections. The game-like story line for the **Absurd Math** pre-algebra activities centers on a group of evil scientists in a futuristic city. Through the four episodes, the problem-solving grows progressively more challenging. Select **Printable Worksheets** to be taken to several engaging exercises that build on algebra skills. The **Puzzle of the Week** takes us back to pre-algebra, while the **Skill Builders and Challenges** section focuses on area and perimeter of common plane figures.

One word of caution to teachers of students with low proficiency in reading or English language skills: the reading level of much of this material can be challenging. The use of teen slang and non-standard English may pose a problem for students who struggle with reading comprehension.

# Math Forum@Drexel

## mathforum.org

**SITE DESCRIPTION:** This superlative Web site contains invaluable resources for students, parents, educators, and researchers. Have a question about math? **Ask Dr. Math** by submitting it to "him" or "her" (actually a group of graduate students), or browse the archive of previously submitted questions. Need to find a new problem to challenge your students with? Visit the **Problem of the Week** sections for a vast array of possibilities. In **Teacher2Teacher**, teachers and parents can discuss topics related to teaching mathematics. **Math Resources by Subject** offers a guide to the best Internet resources on mathematical topics for K–12, college, and advanced users.

To get started on Math Forum@Drexel, click on the **Quick Reference** box near the bottom of the home page. You're taken to a neatly organized matrix that lays out all the site's main features. Visitors may also subscribe to a free e-mail newsletter.

**HIGHLIGHTS FOR TEACHERS:** This site has so many fabulous resources, it's difficult to single out just a few. In the **MathTools** sections, topics are identified by grade level, and links are given to interactive online teaching tools, lesson plans, and further activities. In the right-hand column on the **MathTools** page, you'll even find links to stories involving math. Don't miss the Technology POWs, which are interactive challenge activities that create extensions from the Problems of the Week. Look for the buttons at the top of the home page that will take you to separate areas for middle and high school students (**Student Center**) and middle and high school teachers (**Teachers' Place**).

---

**Math Forum Quick Reference**

Who Are You?

What Topic Interests You?

Need Lessons, Software & Activities?

Carve Your Own Set of Math Resources

Discussions and Public Forums

Interactive Projects at the Math Forum

Special Projects & Hard-to-Find Favorites

About Us; How to Participate; Navigation

**Show Quick Reference Sheet again**

### The Math Forum @ Drexel — DONATE

### Quick Reference Sheet

| Main Areas | Projects | Features | Archives |
|---|---|---|---|
| Search for Math Resources | Ask Dr. Math | Dynamic Geometry Software | Articles & Book Reviews |
| Student Center | Teacher2Teacher | Teacher Exchange | Geometry Newsgroup / Topics |
| Teachers' Place | Math Fundamentals Problem of the Week | Internet Math Library | Internet Software: Mac \| PC |
| Parents & Citizens | Pre-Algebra Problem of the Week | Math Forum Newsletter | Learning & Math Discussions |
| Research Division | Geometry Problem of the Week | Mathematics Discussion Groups | Mailing Lists & Newsgroups |
| Math Resources by Subject | Algebra Problem of the Week | Math Awareness Month | Math Software |
| Math Education | Active Problem Library | Math Forum Showcase | *Mathematics Teacher* Bibliographies |
| Key Issues in Math | MathTools | What's New? | Math Forum Workshops |

**Privacy Policy**

Suggestion Box \|\| Home \|\| The Math Library \|\| Help Desk \|\| Quick Reference \|\| Search

© 1994-2004 The Math Forum
http://mathforum.org/
The Math Forum is a research and educational enterprise of Drexel University.

## Mathematics Materials for Tomorrow's Teachers

**www.mste.uiuc.edu/m2t2/**

**SITE DESCRIPTION:** Mathematics Materials for Tomorrow's Teachers (M2T2) covers the entire gamut of middle school mathematics. Developed by teachers, administrators, university researchers, mathematicians, graduate students, and members of the Illinois State Board of Education, this Web site offers "interesting, mathematically rich, challenging, and appropriate" activities that map effectively to the Illinois state mathematics standards and its achievement testing program.

At the center of M2T2 are five mathematics resource modules created for inservice training of middle school teachers. The modules address **Number Sense**, **Measurement**, **Algebra**, **Geometry**, and **Statistics**. The modules are complete and very explicit, walking teachers through a variety of problem sets and activities (hands-on, paper-and-pencil, and online).

**HIGHLIGHTS FOR TEACHERS:** To access the modules, click on **M2T2 Files** in the left-hand navigation menu, answer the short survey, then proceed to the download page. The modules are available in both PDF and Microsoft Publisher (PUB) format. The yellow box contains the middle school modules. Teachers can use the modules as a source for lesson plans and for enrichment and extension activities. Don't miss the **Resources** link in the navigation menu; it takes visitors to a select list of Web sites that explore number sense, measurement, algebra, geometry, and statistics.

Another valuable resource is the excellent collection of Java applets, developed at the University of Illinois, to illustrate many of the concepts in the program. Clicking on **Applets** (under **Home**) in the navigation menu takes you to a list of applets that correspond to the modules. What's more, the first link takes you to a list of 65 more applets for mathematics and science education. While on this page, be sure to check out **Lessons & Curriculum** in the left-hand navigation bar.

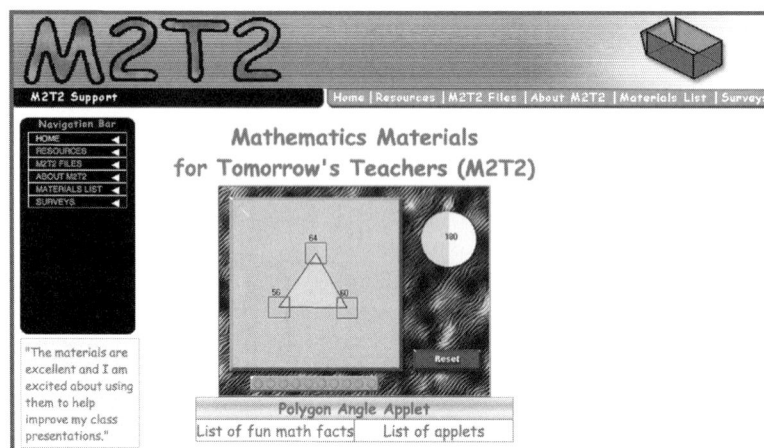

## National Library of Virtual Manipulatives for Interactive Mathematics

matti.usu.edu/nlvm/nav/

**SITE DESCRIPTION:** This elegant Web site gathers dozens and dozens of interactive manipulatives designed to accompany the National Council of Teachers of Mathematics (NCTM) standards and help students visualize mathematical relationships and applications. All grade levels are addressed.

The manipulatives are divided into groups that address **Number & Operations**, **Algebra**, **Geometry**, **Measurement**, and **Data Analysis & Probability**. Click on **Virtual Library** and you are taken to a simple matrix that clusters these topics into grade bands for **Pre-K–2**, **3–5**, **6–8**, and **9–12**. In the index, each manipulative is named and briefly described. Most of the manipulatives come with instructions for several activities and are keyed to the NCTM standards.

**HIGHLIGHTS FOR TEACHERS:** Use these fabulous teaching aids with an LCD projector, SmartBoard or large-screen monitor to enliven your instruction and motivate students to new levels of understanding and participation.

Some of the best manipulatives include **Ladybug Leaf** and **Ladybug Mazes** in the **Geometry** section. They provide a basic introduction to programming. The **Attribute Blocks** and **Geoboards** are loads of fun, and **Grapher**, in the **Algebra** section, enables users to dynamically graph and explore functions. Veteran teachers will be pleased to see their old friends **Pattern Blocks** and **Pentominoes** in a new setting here. Don't be fooled by this site's simple graphics: you'll find plenty of useful material here!

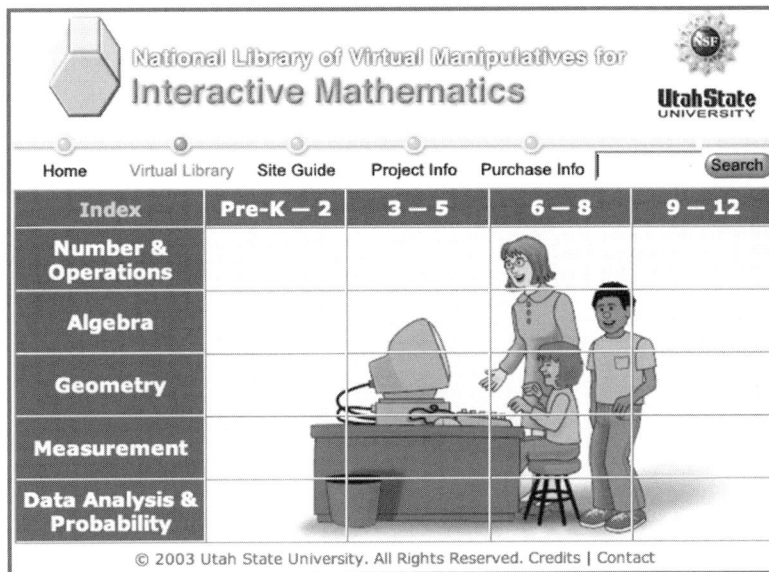

## Problems with a Point
### www2.edc.org/mathproblems/

**SITE DESCRIPTION:** Problems with a Point comes from the Education Development Center. It's designed for students in Grades 6–12 and offers a collection of conceptually linked problem sequences that focus on basic mathematical ideas and the connections between them. Nearly 300 problems are housed on the site; each one builds on students' prior knowledge, using various tools and approaches and functioning at different levels of difficulty. Answers and solutions are provided, and many problems include hints. To make it easy for teachers to find problems or problem sets that support their curriculum, synopses of each problem in the collection are searchable by keyword. In addition, visitors may select groups of problems by topic, time required, suggested technology, required mathematical background, and learning style.

**HIGHLIGHTS FOR TEACHERS:** From the home page, click on **Mathematics Problems**. From here, you'll find Math **Topics** listed, including Math Without Math; Number; Geometry and Measurement; Algebra and Functions; Statistics and Probability; Discrete Mathematics; Trigonometry; Logic, Axiomatic Systems, and Foundations; Topology; and Calculus. Extensive guides are included to make teacher use of the site as easy and productive as possible.

A sample problem named "What goes up, must come down #2" asks students to make predictions and analyze data (in both graphical and numerical form) to determine the angle a ball should be thrown to obtain maximum horizontal distance. The somewhat surprising answer? It all depends on the height from which the ball is thrown.

## Shodor Education Foundation

**www.shodor.org**

**SITE DESCRIPTION:** The Shodor Education Foundation was founded in 1994 with a mission "to advance science and math education through the use of computational science, modeling, and technology." In support of this mission, the organization has developed a Web site with a range of tools and activities for every age group, from elementary school to graduate school to professional practitioners. The site is divided into three main sections: **Curriculum Materials**, **Faculty Development**, and **Student Enrichment**.

After choosing **Curriculum Materials**, select **All Projects** from the navigation menu on the right to access a list of projects. The projects likely to be of most interest to secondary-level educators are Project Interactivate, Computation Science Education Reference Desk (CSERD), ChemViz Curriculum Support Services, MASTER Tools, SUCCEED-HI (computational science resources for the hearing impaired, with ASL video), and the UNC-Chapel Hill Fundamentals Program.

**HIGHLIGHTS FOR TEACHERS:** Project Interactivate is the foundation's best-known and most widely applicable initiative. It focuses on concepts in numbers and operations, geometry and measurement, functions and algebra, and probability and data analysis, incorporating more than 100 activities and more than three-dozen tools. All activities are keyed to the standards of the National Council of Teachers of Mathematics and the National Council on Economic Education. The project cross-indexes each activity with seven of the most widely used math textbook series, so teachers can easily integrate these specifically designed applets into their existing curricula.

The UNC-Chapel Hill Fundamentals program reviews the fundamentals of chemistry for first-year chemistry students. ChemViz offers computer simulations and visualization tools. CSERD houses a collection of activities, models, tutorials, applications, and algorithms for use in physics, mathematics, astronomy, and biology. Activities and models come with lessons or software.

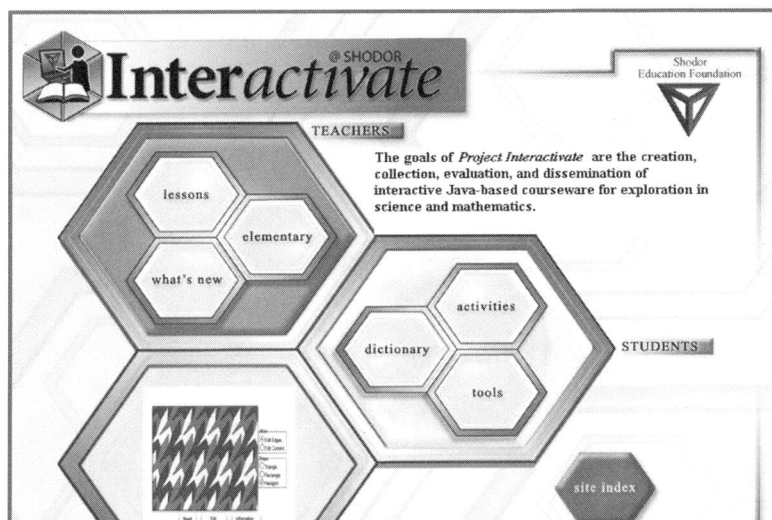

## Tools for Understanding

**www.ups.edu/community/tofu/**

**SITE DESCRIPTION:** Middle and high school teachers of special education and remedial math know very well the topics covered on the Web site Tools for Understanding (ToFU for short). They're the same topics students wrestle with year after year: fractions, decimals, geometry, functions, and problem solving. ToFU presents an alternative approach to teaching these problem areas by employing a variety of technologies (primarily spreadsheets and calculators, along with writing) to build supplementary activities and materials. The overall approach is conceptual, but activities are anchored in everyday contexts as much as possible.

ToFU is composed of three strands: **Math Concepts, Integrated Lessons,** and **Journaling.** In **Math Concepts,** the lessons are designed to extend students' mathematical understanding through both visualization and the application of math to everyday settings. The **Integrated Lessons** strand integrates technology with mathematical problem solving and written communication. **Journaling** encourages students to reflect on and articulate their own thinking process. It also helps make abstract concepts concrete while giving teachers valuable information about how their students are learning math. ToFU is designed to supplement, not replace, a good math textbook and curriculum. The activities were developed and field-tested extensively by researchers at the University of Puget Sound through a grant from the U.S. Department of Education.

**HIGHLIGHTS FOR TEACHERS:** The organization and presentation of the **Math Concepts** problems is precise and orderly. The use of spreadsheets and calculators removes much of the computational difficulty that can get in the way of student understanding. The authors of ToFU explain their approach by pointing out that "the nature of student failure in secondary mathematics...must be viewed in the context of what [basic skills drills] mean to the students we teach. Learning to do complex long division problems by hand is likely to have little personal or social value to an eighth-grader who is only taking mathematics because he or she is required to." The tips and strategies in the **Journaling** strand make a great deal of sense and are presented in a manner that addresses the anxiety that many math teachers may have about writing.

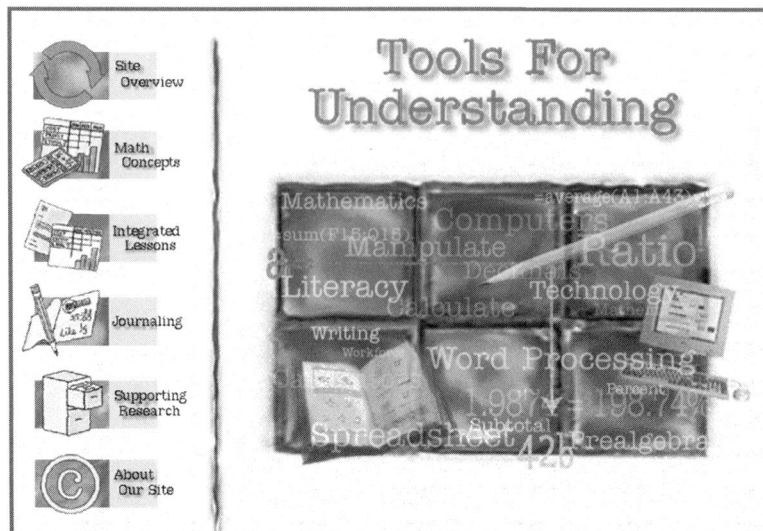

# CHAPTER 7

# Science

Secondary Science teachers will find plenty in this chapter to support their instructional planning and delivery. Many of these Web sites employ applets and other forms of interactivity to illustrate, clarify, and demonstrate important concepts and functions. Such sites include Biology in Motion, Howard Hughes Medical Institute's BioInteractive, PhysicsLessons.com, and Physics Applets. Other sites, such as ActionBioscience.org, American Field Guide, and Exploratorium, use on-demand video effectively. ActionBioscience.org even pays teachers to write lesson plans. Three of the sites—National Science Teachers Association, Exploratorium, and Chemistry.org—publish magazines to provide teachers with current news, activities, lesson plans, tips, and ideas. Current and back issues of these magazines are archived online.

PhysicsLessons.com offers an online whiteboard to draw diagrams, chat, and share images in real time. NASA Education Enterprise serves as a portal to more than 24 educational sites developed and maintained by various arms of the space agency. The Why Files publishes weekly articles on the real science behind news headlines, and ESTME Web Site Gallery highlights 45 of the best science-related educational Web sites as judged by the National Science Foundation and the U.S. Department of Education. Finally, one site in this chapter is in a category all its own. The Comic Book Periodic Table of the Elements offers a periodic table like you've never seen before, complete with all your favorite comic book superheroes.

# QUICK REFERENCE CHART

| Science | FEATURES FOR TEACHERS | | | | | | |
|---|---|---|---|---|---|---|---|
| Name of Site/URL | chat or forum | lesson plans | teacher resources | parent resources | teacher's guide | video, audio, applets | Web links |
| ActionBioscience.org<br>www.actionbioscience.org | | | | | | | |
| American Field Guide<br>www.pbs.org/americanfieldguide/ | | | | | | | |
| Biology in Motion<br>biologyinmotion.com | | | | | | | |
| Chemistry.org<br>www.chemistry.org | | | | | | | |
| The Comic Book Periodic Table of the Elements<br>www.uky.edu/Projects/Chemcomics/ | | | | | | | |
| ESTME Web Site Gallery<br>www.estme.org/gallery/ | | | | | | | |
| Exploratorium<br>www.exploratorium.edu | | | | | | | |
| Howard Hughes Medical Institute's BioInteractive<br>www.biointeractive.org | | | | | | | |
| NASA Education Enterprise<br>www.education.nasa.gov | | | | | | | |
| National Science Teachers Association<br>www.nsta.org | | | | | | | |
| Physical Sciences Resource Center<br>psrc.aapt.org | | | | | | | |
| Physics Applets<br>jersey.uoregon.edu/vlab/ | | | | | | | |
| PhysicsLessons.com<br>www.physicslessons.com | | | | | | | |
| The Why Files<br>whyfiles.org | | | | | | | |

The shaded boxes indicate the feature is available on the Web site.

# QUICK REFERENCE CHART *(continued)*

| Science | FEATURES FOR TEACHERS | | | FEATURES FOR STUDENTS | | |
|---|---|---|---|---|---|---|
| Name of Site/URL | assessment ideas | e-newsletter | reproducibles | activities | interactive exercises | reading material |
| **ActionBioscience.org** www.actionbioscience.org | | Update | | | | |
| **American Field Guide** www.pbs.org/americanfieldguide/ | | | | | | |
| **Biology in Motion** biologyinmotion.com | | | | | | |
| **Chemistry.org** www.chemistry.org | | E-mail Alerts | | | | |
| **The Comic Book Periodic Table of the Elements** www.uky.edu/Projects/Chemcomics/ | | | | | | |
| **ESTME Web Site Gallery** www.estme.org/gallery/ | | | | | | |
| **Exploratorium** www.exploratorium.edu | | eNews | | | | |
| **Howard Hughes Medical Institute's BioInteractive** www.biointeractive.org | | | | | | |
| **NASA Education Enterprise** www.education.nasa.gov | | Express Mailing List | | | | |
| **National Science Teachers Association** www.nsta.org | | NSTA Express (weekly), Science Class (monthly) | | | | |
| **Physical Sciences Resource Center** psrc.aapt.org | | | | | | |
| **Physics Applets** jersey.uoregon.edu/vlab/ | | | | | | |
| **PhysicsLessons.com** www.physicslessons.com | | PhysicsLessons Newsletter | | | | |
| **The Why Files** whyfiles.org | | Science Behind the News | | | | |

The shaded boxes indicate the feature is available on the Web site.

# ActionBioscience.org

### www.actionbioscience.org

**SITE DESCRIPTION:** The American Institute of Biological Sciences (AIBS) maintains this Web site through a grant from the National Science Foundation. The centerpiece is a continually updated collection of topical, accessible articles on a wide range of biological topics. The articles are categorized into seven high-priority areas: **Biodiversity**, **Environment**, **Genomics**, **Biotechnology**, **Evolution**, **New Frontiers**, and **Education**.

Original lessons (intended for students from middle school to college) have been written to accompany many of the articles on ActionBioscience. K–12 educators can actually receive an honorarium if the lessons they write for the site are accepted. At the end of each article, links appear that connect readers who want to learn more or get involved. Some articles are also translated into Spanish. The site publishes a free e-mail newsletter and maintains an update service to notify readers when new materials are added in areas of expressed interest.

**HIGHLIGHTS FOR TEACHERS:** Most teachers will want to start by browsing through the growing **Lesson Directory**. Lessons are peer-reviewed and keyed to the National Science Education Standards. Lessons contain a number of activities and are directly related to the articles they accompany. The site also gives educators access to on-demand videos of key presentations at AIBS conferences. Click on the white box that reads **View AIBS lectures online**, at the very top of the home page, to go to this virtual library.

## American Field Guide

www.pbs.org/americanfieldguide/

**SITE DESCRIPTION:** Oregon Public Broadcasting (OPB), in partnership with the Public Broadcasting Service (PBS), has gathered film and video of the American outdoors from nearly 30 member stations across the country. OPB has made it all available on this Web site, online and on-demand. The video streams are high-resolution and uniformly excellent. Visitors may search the collection by keyword, topic, and state. Topics include **Animals**, **Ecosystems**, **Human History**, **Livelihoods**, **Earth & Space**, **Plants**, **Public Policy**, and **Recreation**. Hundreds of videos are available, from short clips to entire PBS programs.

**HIGHLIGHTS FOR TEACHERS:** American Field Guide provides great support in its **Teacher Resources** section. Visitors will find 19 Units of Inquiry that gather video segments on specific topics. They're accompanied by lesson plans that include background, content standards, extension Web sites, and several activities. The units are briefly described and the intended grade levels are indicated. Samples of topics for the units include fires, floods, forests, insects, landfills, ocean habitats, the rock cycle, and volcanoes.

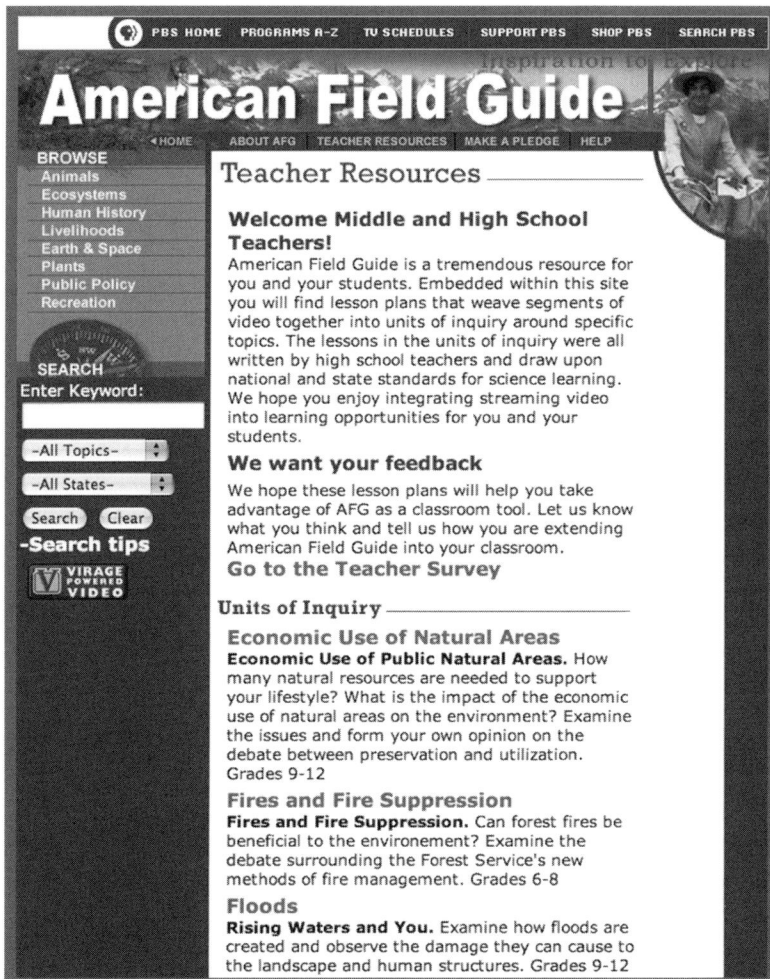

## Biology in Motion

**biologyinmotion.com**

**SITE DESCRIPTION:** Biology in Motion offers highly engaging, creative, and clever interactives to illustrate basic processes and concepts in biology. The Web site is the brainchild of Leif Saul, who appears to have created everything on the site—artwork, words, and the programming code. What a job well done!

Most of the interactives require a browser with the Flash plug-in. The animations, activities, and cartoons are accompanied by clear and succinct explanations. As of this writing, Biology in Motion contains nine activities and exhibits.

**HIGHLIGHTS FOR TEACHERS:** Dr. Saul provides a number of meaningful **Tips for Teachers** regarding how to use his creations to maximize their effects on student learning. Topics addressed include **Intestinal Gas**, **Enzyme Characteristics**, **Organize-It** interactive study aid, **ATP and Energy Storage**, **Fat Digestion and Bile**, **The Cardiovascular System**, and **Urine Concentration in 3 Easy Steps**. **Evolution Lab** is particularly fascinating; students can easily simulate the effects of selection, mutation, and chance on the evolution of a particular heritable trait.

# Chemistry.org

## www.chemistry.org

**SITE DESCRIPTION:** This home page for the American Chemical Society offers a great deal of material for teachers and students, as well as resources for chemistry professionals, enthusiasts, and policy makers. Click on **Educators & Students** on the home page. You'll be taken to a page with links and descriptions of the American Chemical Society's activities and materials.

On this page, **Re:Source Chemistry** provides numerous activities for middle school chemistry classrooms, along with background information. Many activities are given for **Acids & Bases**, **Density**, **Environment**, **The Language of Chemistry**, **Matter**, and **Chemical Reactions**. Additional topics are promised for the future.

**HIGHLIGHTS FOR TEACHERS:** At the high school level, visitors will find information about the **Chemagination** science essay competition and the **Chemistry Olympiad** national competition. Teachers will also be interested in **VC2: The Virtual Chemistry Club** and **ChemMatters** print magazine, which covers chemistry in everyday life. VC2 contains a large collection of enjoyable and informative articles and activities on such topics as the chemical composition of artificial snow, Cheese Whiz, new car smell, and teeth whiteners.

*ChemMatters,* published quarterly, includes numerous lively pieces about the field. A teacher's guide accompanies each issue, with additional information about articles, hands-on activities, classroom demonstrations, and other resources. Copies of the current and past issues and teacher's guides are available online, going back to 2002. Visitors may also register to receive a free monthly e-mail newsletter.

## The Comic Book Periodic Table of the Elements
**www.uky.edu/Projects/Chemcomics/**

**SITE DESCRIPTION:** You've probably never seen a periodic table of the elements quite like this one. The site's creators—John P. Selegue and F. James Holler, both from the Department of Chemistry at the University of Kentucky—clearly had too much time on their hands when they were growing up. Nearly every element in the table is accompanied by at least one comic book panel, and sometimes many. If you click on a panel, you can view the whole comic book page. In most cases, there's actually some tidbit of scientific information in the comic about that particular element, as well as a good deal of esoteric information about the provenance of the comic.

**HIGHLIGHTS FOR TEACHERS:** Click on the name of any element, and you're taken to its own page. In the upper left-hand corner, you'll see a color-coded square with rounded corners and the element's symbol and periodic numbers. If you click on it, you'll be taken to the corresponding page for the element on a site called Mark Winter's Web Elements, reputed to be the first periodic table on the Web.

# ESTME Web Site Gallery

**www.estme.org/gallery/**

**SITE DESCRIPTION:** ESTME stands for Excellence in Science, Technology, and Mathematics Education. A week is set aside annually to recognize exemplary programs, projects, and organizations in these areas. The agencies behind ESTME are the National Science Foundation and the U.S. Department of Education.

You can find an outstanding collection of links and pages in nine different areas of the Gallery: **Numbers**, **Living Things**, **Earth and Environment**, **Physical World**, **Machines and Inventions**, **Human Mind and Culture**, **Human Body**, **The Universe**, and **Science Collections**.

**HIGHLIGHTS FOR TEACHERS:** Each of the nine areas listed above highlights five Web sites, selected for their quality and relevance to K–12 education. For example, the **Game Theory** site describes how mathematical concepts underlie the plots in popular films, literature, and headline news stories. **Backyard Jungle** enables users to create maps of the nature surrounding them and chart the animals and plants they see. **Invention at Play** offers interactive exercises that teach problem solving and visual thinking. **Make Up Your Mind** focuses on brain anatomy and function.

Click on **Ask a Scientist** to be taken to the National Science Digital Library site, where users can browse more than 300 resource collections devoted to science education. Visitors can also query scientists, engineers, and mathematicians at **AskNSDL**.

**E·S·T·M·E**
Excellence in
Science,
Technology,
and Mathematics
Education
Week

## Web Site Gallery

▸ ESTME WEEK
EVENTS

▸ WEB SITE
GALLERY

  Numbers
  Living Things
  Earth and
  Environment
  Physical World
  Machines and
  Inventions
  Human Mind
  and Culture
  Human Body
  The Universe
  Science
  Collections

▸ LETTER FROM
THE PRESIDENT

▸ ASK A
SCIENTIST

▸ ESTME
PARTNERS

This gallery features award-winning sites that provide a myriad of possibilities for enriching science, technology, and/or mathematics education. Culled from a variety of distinguished institutions, organizations, and individuals, this list is by no means exhaustive. It does, however, provide an excellent sampling of the vast amount of information on the Web. Many of these sites also provide links to other useful resources.

**Numbers**
From abaci to calendars to the geometry of pasta, these sites examine the role of numbers throughout history and in everyday life.

**Living Things**
The diversity of the flora and fauna that surround us is featured in sites exploring such topics as cell biology, migration, and evolution.

**Earth and Environment**
The sky's not the limit with these informative sites: from the stratosphere to your own backyard, discover the fascinating inter-workings of the blue planet.

**Physical World**
Design a virtual roller coaster, find out what's in toothpaste, and explore atomic physics while learning how molecules and energy affect our existence.

**Human Mind and Culture**
Watch a reenactment of an ancient Mesoamerican ballgame, compose music, explore the tombs in the Valley of the Kings, and more.

**Human Body**
Interactive labs and anatomical models teach us how our bodies function, how we are affected by disease, and how we can stay healthy.

**The Universe**
Get a satellite-eye's view of Jupiter, peek through the "eye" of the Hubble telescope, read about the latest astronomical discoveries, and more.

**Science Collections**
Take cybertours of museum exhibits, engage in interactive activities, and discover the science behind the headlines.

## Exploratorium

**www.exploratorium.edu**

**SITE DESCRIPTION:** San Francisco's Exploratorium calls itself "the museum of science, art, and human perception," so you know this is no run-of-the-mill exhibition hall. Indeed, the museum is exceptional. Its Web site is equally so, having won numerous Best of the Web awards around the world. The site is very well organized and easy to navigate. The two areas secondary teachers will be most interested in are **Explore** and **Educate**. **Explore** contains **Online Activities**, **Online Exhibitions**, **Webcasts**, **Hands-on Activities**, **Science News**, an **Online Magazine**, and **Cool Sites**. **Educate** contains some of the same areas, along with **Publications**, an **Educator Newsletter**, and an area for **Professional Development**.

**HIGHLIGHTS FOR TEACHERS:** More than 500 simple experiments can be found in **Hands-on Activities**. These focus on Space, Earth, Sports, Human Body, Mind & Perception, Machines & Tools, Living Things, Society & Culture, and Food. Examples include the famous **Cow's Eye Dissection**, **Brain Explorer**, and **Salt Volcano**. **Online Exhibitions** presents sophisticated uses of technology and covers the same topics as the experiments above, but its experiments are completely different in format and presentation. Some cool samples include **If You're Going to Rob a Bank, Wear a Wig**; **Sheep Brain Dissection**; and the **Visible Human**.

Exploratorium's **Webcasts** are like having your own private library of science videos. More than 100 recorded Webcasts are stored in the archives. Some interesting titles include Interstellar Communication, the Science of Candy, and Echo-Logic. Don't miss the Iron Science Teacher series of Webcasts, in which teachers compete to develop math and science activities in the shortest possible time. They're funny and amazing!

You can sign up for the free e-newsletter or view all back copies online. The newsletter highlights museum activities and exhibits. The museum also publishes a gorgeous, free e-zine for the general public. Finally, Exploratorium has its own list of **Cool Sites**, organized into 23 subject categories that include arts, earth science, invention, literature and drama, media, photography, and science literature.

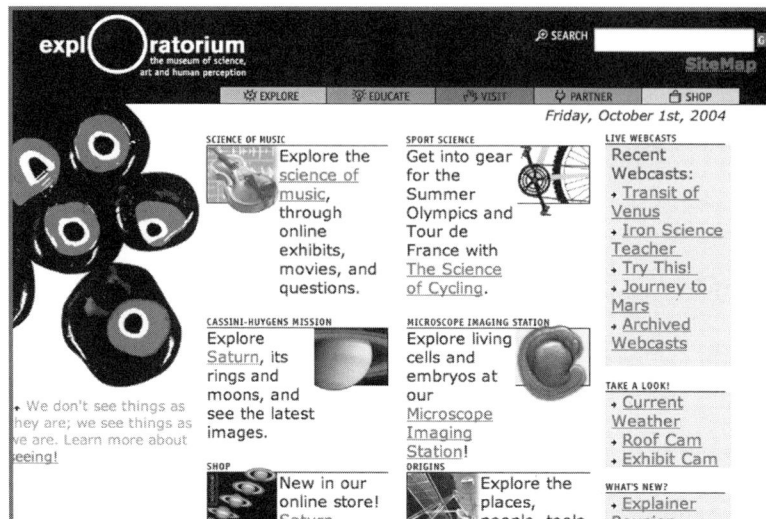

## Howard Hughes Medical Institute's BioInteractive
**www.biointeractive.org**

**SITE DESCRIPTION:** BioInteractive offers visitors a marvelously rich and informative learning experience. Its lavish use of animation, virtual labs, and video makes it easy and entertaining to access. Its academic content is of the highest quality.

Holiday Lectures in Science is the centerpiece of this Web site. Aimed primarily at high school honors and AP biology students and their teachers, the **Lectures** are designed to provide students and teachers an opportunity to learn about cutting-edge research from some of the world's leading scientists. They are also designed to inspire young people to pursue careers in science. Each lecture is available for on-demand viewing online or in DVD format, free upon request. Additional resource materials relevant for general biology students and middle schoolers are available to accompany the lectures. Recent topics have included cancer, neuro-science, genes and gender, proteins and small molecules, and discoveries in biological time. The lectures and their accompanying materials are listed in a vertical toolbar on the left-hand side of the home page.

**HIGHLIGHTS FOR TEACHERS:** You'll find far more here than just lectures on video. More than three-dozen animations support learning in such topics as immunology, infectious diseases, hearts and hypertension, and DNA. The **Virtual Labs** section is truly outstanding, having won best-in-the-world honors among more than 1,200 entries in the Pirelli International Award competition. It won a similar Sci-Tech Web Award from *Scientific American*. Each virtual lab consists of introductory materials, an online notebook, quizzes, additional resources, and help. In these labs, students actually engage in experiments on such topics as the transgenic fly, bacterial identification, cardiology, and neurophysiology.

BioInteractive also includes an **Ask a Scientist** service, a **Virtual Museum** with four exhibits, and a direct link to the site **DNAi** (DNAinteractive). DNAi explores DNA in great detail and hosts a collection of resources to rival BioInteractive's. The site also offers teachers a place to post their personal Web sites, all for free.

## NASA Education Enterprise
www.education.nasa.gov

**SITE DESCRIPTION:** NASA maintains more than two-dozen education Web sites, each with its own content. This can make finding just what you want a bit difficult. Fortunately, NASA Education Enterprise serves as an umbrella site that brings it all together. The red box at the top left-hand side of the home page is a good place to start; hyperlinks are labeled **For Kids**, **For Students**, **For Educators**, and **Education News**. **For Students** is divided into grade levels and contains homework help, Internet resources, multimedia resources, and learning opportunities. **For Educators** offers features, news, learning resources, Internet resources, multimedia resources, contacts, professional development, and student opportunities.

Another useful point of entry is the **NASA Education Offices** box in the gray toolbar at the top of the home page. The link **Elementary & Secondary Education** will take you to descriptions of NASA educational programs. From there, clicking on **Contacts** will give you the names of people in your area who are responsible for many different types of educational outreach. Click on **Center Offices** to get a list of the 10 NASA centers that maintain education sites. Click on **Enterprise Offices** to locate five more NASA entities that maintain education sites.

**HIGHLIGHTS FOR TEACHERS:** Most online content for teachers and students is located in **Center Offices** and **Enterprise Offices**. There you'll find activities, lesson plans, newsletters, and curriculum materials about such specific areas as aeronautics and space technology; the Earth, its environment, the solar system, and the universe; robotics; space research and technology commercialization; and human space exploration.

To view some of NASA's great pictures, users may go to **Earth Science Picture of the Day** at **epod.usra.edu**, the NASA Image Exchange at **nix.nasa.gov**, or Great Images in NASA at **grin.hq.nasa.gov**. Click on NASA Education Programs for a huge number of print resources for educators and students. Visitors may search for programs by subject, center of origin, or grade level.

## National Science Teachers Association

### www.nsta.org

**SITE DESCRIPTION:** Most membership organizations provide lots of services for those who belong and very few for those who don't. Fortunately, the National Science Teachers Association (NSTA) has numerous partners to help defray the cost of giving help to anyone who asks for it. Its Web site offers a tremendous amount of support to science teachers at any grade level.

The Your Classroom buttons on the home page are an excellent place to start. Choose **High School** to be taken to a page that includes news; excerpts from NSTA's professional journal, *Science Teacher*; a teachers' discussion board; and links to numerous resources for high schools. Check the vertical toolbar on the left for links to the rest of the Web site.

**HIGHLIGHTS FOR TEACHERS:** Click on **Teacher Resources** to access the *Science Class* electronic newsletter, which publishes monthly guides based on grade level for use by science teachers. You can also find here the **SciLinks** guide to useful Web sites keyed to your particular science textbook, as well as the **Science Websites** page, with its searchable database of recommended Web sites.

An even better feature can be found in **Professional Info** under **NSTA Science Guides**. Each science guide is broken down into themes, contains a list of Web resources and case studies for teachers and students, and offers lesson plans that integrate all this information. Grades 5–8 themes include organisms, community, ecosystems, and environment. Grades 9–12 themes include nonrenewable energy and renewable resources, impacts of energy use, and applications of technology. This is an outstanding and imaginative use of the power of the Internet!

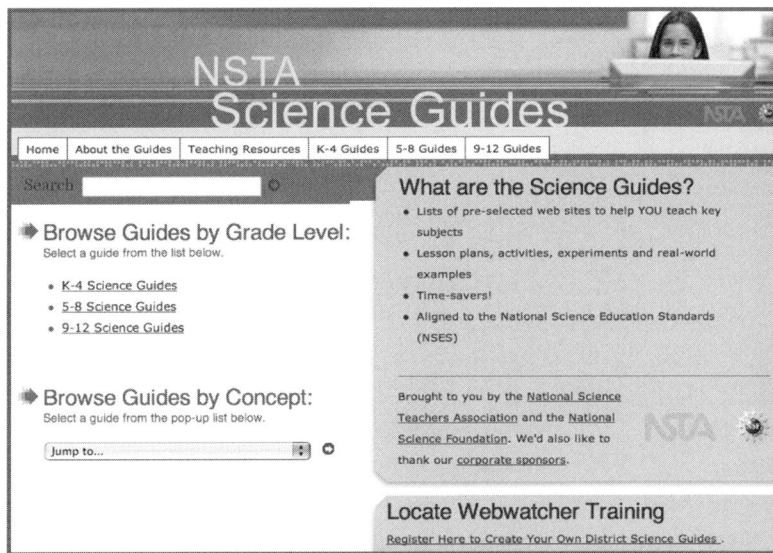

## Physical Sciences Resource Center

### psrc.aapt.org

**SITE DESCRIPTION:** The Physical Sciences Resource Center Web site is produced by the American Association of Physics Teachers. It houses a growing and searchable collection of resources in 11 areas of physical science, such as astronomy, mechanics, physics, optics, and thermodynamics. Materials for all ages (from elementary to graduate school) are provided. Teacher resources (click on **Browse Resource Types**) fall into seven areas: **Assessment**, **Collections**, **Curriculum**, **Event**, **Instructor Reference**, **Lectures & Demos**, and **Research**. Student resources also are provided in seven areas: **Activity**, **Animation**, **Drill & Practice**, **Laboratory**, **Simulation**, **Student Reference**, and **Tutorial**.

**HIGHLIGHTS FOR TEACHERS:** Resources on this site may be free, or they may be downloadable for a nominal fee. A convenient feature on the site is **My Filing Cabinet**, where you can collect your resources and hold them for future reference. Visitors need to register (for free) to use this function.

## Physics Applets

**jersey.uoregon.edu/vlab/**

**SITE DESCRIPTION:** This set of more than 40 interactive applets has been prepared for use in physics, astronomy, and environmental science courses. The site is hosted by the Department of Physics at the University of Oregon.

The **Astrophysics** group of applets focuses on spectroscopy, photometry, orbital mechanics, and cosmology. Those in **Energy & Environment** cover the greenhouse effect, weather, exponential growth, voltage, work, population growth, units of math, length and time, and electrical circuits. The **Mechanics** collection delves into 1D and 2D motion, friction, and energy conservation, while **Thermodynamics** includes displays on the piston, the balloon, and the first law. Java-based tools are also provided to help students make graphs, figures, and spreadsheets.

**HIGHLIGHTS FOR TEACHERS:** These applets are ideal for projection from your computer for whole-class or large-group teaching. If you're fortunate enough to have a Smartboard or similar device, students can actually manipulate data and control the interactive examples with their hands on the screen. These applets will enrich the learning environment, whether they are used in a setting for large groups, small groups, or individual study.

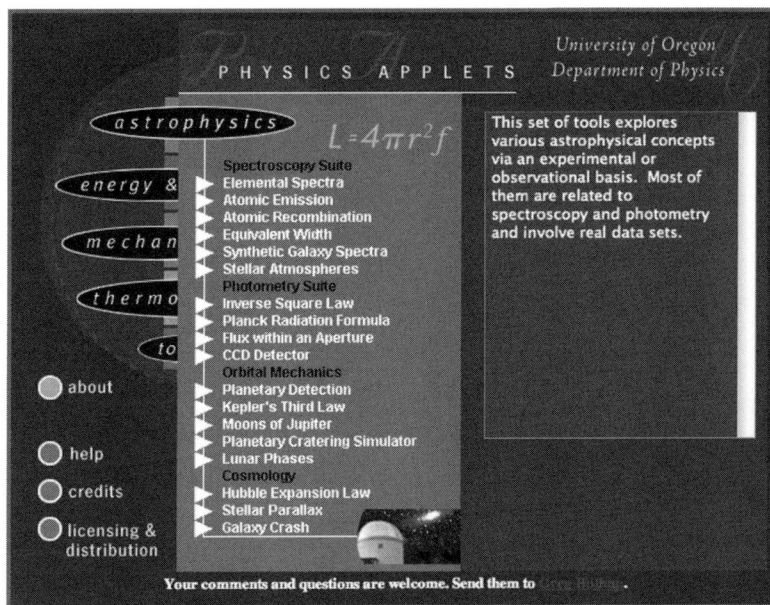

## PhysicsLessons.com
### www.physicslessons.com

**SITE DESCRIPTION:** Here's a great Web site for high school physics teachers, built and maintained by Jeff Whittaker, a high school physics teacher himself. The site is filled with experiments, simulations, tools, and animations, designed to demonstrate key concepts. Visitors can even set up their own e-mail account on the site, and everything is free.

The home page provides easy access to all areas of PhysicsLessons.com: **News**, **Demonstrations** (animated), **iPhysics** (interactive lab simulations), **X-Labs** (complete lab experiments), **News** (daily news feed), **Q-Physics** (questions to probe understanding), **Quiz Zone** (quizzes that grade themselves automatically), and a free monthly e-mail newsletter.

**HIGHLIGHTS FOR TEACHERS:** A nice feature is **WhiteBoard**, where visitors can draw diagrams, chat, and share images in real time; the link is in the bottom left-hand corner of the home page. Near the **WhiteBoard** link, visitors will also find a link to the active **PhysicsForums**, which hosts nearly four-dozen discussion groups. The reference tools—**Graphic Calculator**, **Calculator**, **Stopwatch**, **Unit Converter**, **Equations**, **Phys. Constants**, an interactive **Periodic Table Shop**, and a course on HTML (**Learn HTML**), among others—are all easy to use, and helpful.

## The Why Files

**whyfiles.org**

**SITE DESCRIPTION:** This is a simple, clean, and well-organized Web site. Each week, The Why Files publishes a new, illustrated article on the science behind the headlines. The stories have compelling graphics, are written in plain English, and cover their topics well—and with a certain sense of humor. Generally speaking, topics addressed include science, health, environment, and technology. Material is organized for students in Grades 5–8 or 9–12.

The home page changes weekly and offers stories In Depth, In Brief, and In the News. Don't miss the two sections on the bottom right-hand side titled Interactives and Cool Science Images.

The Why Files has four interactive animations on tornadoes, lightning, snowflakes, and baseball. Cool Science Images contains dozens of dramatic photographs dealing with biology, earth and space, environment, health, physical science, and technology.

**HIGHLIGHTS FOR TEACHERS:** The Why Files' designers understand the importance of easy navigation, so this site offers several ways to search through the more than 200 archived articles. For ease of browsing the Grades 5–8 area, articles are organized into such topics as physical science, life science, science as inquiry, earth and space science, science and technology, science in personal and social perspectives, and history and nature of science. The Grades 9–12 area contains more than 38 standards-based topics. Another way to locate articles is to click on **Archives** in the toolbar at the top of the home page. This takes users to areas where they can browse by subject or by theme.

# CHAPTER 8

# Social Studies

This chapter contains a cavalcade of cool Web resources for social studies teachers, ranging from current events to ancient history. You can interact online (or on the phone) with subject area experts at Newsweek Education Program. At the Center for History and New Media, the Internet History Sourcebooks Project, and Digital History, visitors can locate specialized histories of such topics as film, ethnicity, private life, science, medicine, Islam, Judaism, courtship, and decision making.

If you like the online virtual exhibits that can be browsed at Humanities-Interactive, you can borrow the real ones and bring them to your school for only a nominal shipping cost. HyperHistory Online outlines 3,000 years of world history in a single graphic organizer. Take virtual excursions or view virtual exhibits at The Learning Page and National Geographic Education Guide. Students can climb on the Cyberschoolbus to study interactive units on workers' rights as well as the development of cities, peace, poverty, and human rights. They may use multimedia resources to investigate more than 50 of history's most notable trials at the Web site Famous Trials. Visitors can select from more than 160 projects in responsible social activism at iEARN. The site Special Projects: Understanding World Events helps teachers create structures for students to explore crises, war, discrimination, and 9/11. Teachers will find an unending supply of unique resources at History/Social Studies for K–12 Teachers, including a mummy-wrapping exercise, a virtual walking tour of Venice, and the Web's best collection of links on diversity. Finally, hundreds of lesson plans, unit plans, and other robust resources are located at SCORE: History/Social Science.

# QUICK REFERENCE CHART

| Social Studies | FEATURES FOR TEACHERS | | | | | | |
|---|---|---|---|---|---|---|---|
| Name of Site/URL | chat or forum | lesson plans | teacher resources | parent resources | teacher's guide | video, audio, applets | Web links |
| Center for History and New Media<br>chnm.gmu.edu | | | | | | | |
| Cyberschoolbus: United Nations<br>www.cyberschoolbus.un.org | | | | | | | |
| Digital History<br>www.digitalhistory.uh.edu | | | | | | | |
| Famous Trials<br>www.law.umkc.edu/faculty/projects/ftrials/ftrials.htm | | | | | | | |
| History/Social Studies for K–12 Teachers<br>home.comcast.net/~dboals1/boals.html | | | | | | | |
| Humanities-Interactive<br>www.humanities-interactive.org/a_base_UD.html | | | | | | | |
| HyperHistory Online<br>www.hyperhistory.com/online_n2/History_n2/a.html | | | | | | | |
| iEARN<br>www.iearn.org | | | | | | | |
| Internet History Sourcebooks Project<br>www.fordham.edu/halsall/ | | | | | | | |
| The Learning Page . . . Especially for Teachers<br>lcweb2.loc.gov/learn/ | | | | | | | |
| National Geographic Education Guide<br>www.nationalgeographic.com/education/ | | | | | | | |
| Newsweek Education Program<br>www.newsweekeducation.com | *phone service* | | | | | | |
| SCORE: History/Social Science<br>score.rims.k12.ca.us | | | | | | | |
| Special Projects: Understanding World Events<br>www.esrnational.org/sp/we/world.htm | | | | | | | |

The shaded boxes indicate the feature is available on the Web site.

# QUICK REFERENCE CHART *(continued)*

| Social Studies | FEATURES FOR TEACHERS | | | FEATURES FOR STUDENTS | | |
|---|---|---|---|---|---|---|
| Name of Site/URL | assessment ideas | e-newsletter | reproducibles | activities | interactive exercises | reading material |
| **Center for History and New Media** chnm.gmu.edu | | *History News Network* | | | | |
| **Cyberschoolbus: United Nations** www.cyberschoolbus.un.org | | *CyberSchoolBus nEwsMAIL* | | | | |
| **Digital History** www.digitalhistory.uh.edu | | | | | | |
| **Famous Trials** www.law.umkc.edu/faculty/projects/ ftrials/ftrials.htm | | | | | | |
| **History/Social Studies for K–12 Teachers** home.comcast.net/~dboals1/boals.html | | | | | | |
| **Humanities-Interactive** www.humanities-interactive.org/ a_base_UD.html | | | | | | |
| **HyperHistory Online** www.hyperhistory.com/online_n2/ History_n2/a.html | | | | | | |
| **iEARN** www.iearn.org | | *iEARN in Action* | | | | |
| **Internet History Sourcebooks Project** www.fordham.edu/halsall/ | | | | | | |
| **The Learning Page . . . Especially for Teachers** lcweb2.loc.gov/learn/ | | e-mail updates | | | | |
| **National Geographic Education Guide** www.nationalgeographic.com/ education/ | | *Education Update* | | | | |
| **Newsweek Education Program** www.newsweekeducation.com | | *Newsweek ThisWeek Teacher's Guide* | | | | |
| **SCORE: History/Social Science** score.rims.k12.ca.us | | *SCORE H/SS Mailing List* | | | | |
| **Special Projects: Understanding World Events** www.esrnational.org/sp/we/world.htm | | *ESR's e-Newsletter* | | | | |

The shaded boxes indicate the feature is available on the Web site.

## Center for History and New Media

### chnm.gmu.edu

**SITE DESCRIPTION:** This Web site represents a remarkable marriage of scholarship and technology. Its creators at George Mason University have built a marvelously rich collection of fabulous resources. The site is a collaboration between the Center for History and New Media and the American Social History Project/Center for Media and Learning at the Graduate Center of the City University of New York.

The home page for this site invites visitors to follow the paths of its photo links to one of five main areas: **Features**, **History News Network**, **Tools**, **Resources**, and **Projects**. Each area has scholarly essays, original source materials, videos, audio recordings, and new-media tools. Each is designed to enable high school teachers, college and university professors, students, scholars, and the general public to better understand modern events by placing them in historical context. The site's organizers deliberately select historians and writers from a variety of ideological perspectives, to provide balance.

**HIGHLIGHTS FOR TEACHERS:** The resources of most immediate interest to secondary level teachers are in the **Projects** area. Included here are the well-known **History Matters**, a survey course of U.S. History, and the **World History Matters** collection. Both of these areas are full of primary sources, artifacts, and articles from leading experts on how to make and support one's own interpretations of "realia." Other notable sections in **Projects** are **Teaching American History** (lesson plans and project descriptions from high school teachers), **Echo** (a multimedia history of science, technology, and medicine), and **Liberty, Equality, Fraternity** (a multimedia unit on the French Revolution).

Another standout feature of this site is the **History News Network**, an e-zine devoted to consideration of "current events in historical perspective." Visit **Tools** to find **Scribe** (a robust note-taking application), **Survey Builder** ("a tool that builds online surveys, especially applicable to oral histories"), **Scrapbook** (to facilitate creation of collaborative, online scrapbooks), **Poll Builder** (to create online polls), and **Syllabus Finder** (to locate syllabi on a historical topic).

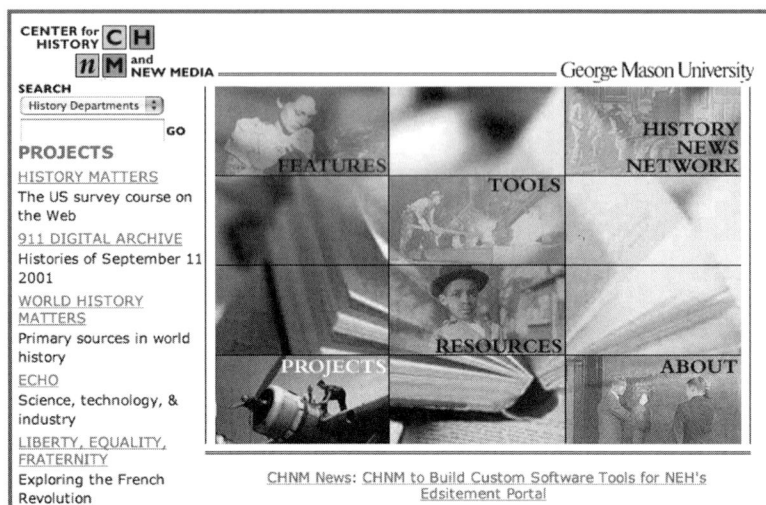

CENTER for CH
HISTORY
and NEW MEDIA — George Mason University
SEARCH
[History Departments ▾]
[_____] GO
**PROJECTS**
HISTORY MATTERS
The US survey course on the Web
911 DIGITAL ARCHIVE
Histories of September 11 2001
WORLD HISTORY MATTERS
Primary sources in world history
ECHO
Science, technology, & industry
LIBERTY, EQUALITY, FRATERNITY
Exploring the French Revolution

FEATURES  TOOLS  HISTORY NEWS NETWORK
RESOURCES
PROJECTS  ABOUT

CHNM News: CHNM to Build Custom Software Tools for NEH's Edsitement Portal

# Cyberschoolbus: United Nations

www.cyberschoolbus.un.org

**SITE DESCRIPTION:** Cyberschoolbus is designed to provide teachers and students with information and teaching materials that pertain to international issues and the United Nations. It aims to create an online global-education community, sponsor action projects to show students how they can impact global problems, and give students a voice on global issues. Everything on Cyberschoolbus is available in English, Spanish, French, Russian, Chinese, and Arabic.

The site is cleanly laid out and easy to navigate. It's divided into four main sections: **Resources, Curriculum, Quizzes & Games**, and **Community**. Clicking on any of these headings will take you to the page for that section, where specific items and projects are described and links posted. Look on the bottom right-hand side of the home page for the blue box labeled **Teachers: Get Free Stuff**. By signing up, you can review or field-test new materials. In the upper right-hand corner find the word **Newsletter** to subscribe to the site's monthly e-mail update.

**HIGHLIGHTS FOR TEACHERS:** Under **Resources**, click on **InfoNation** to view and compare statistical data from country to country. You'll find both **Basic** and **Advanced** versions of this resource. **Country at a Glance** gives a quick overview of statistical information for each country, one at a time. **UN Intro** gives an overview of the history and mission of the United Nations. Within the **Community** section are discussion boards for students, as well as student and professional galleries of photos, artwork, and writing.

For educators, the most useful area of Cyberschoolbus is likely to be the **Curriculum** section, which contains dozens of outstanding thematic units, many with interactive exercises. Two outstanding examples are **Rights at Work**, which explores the importance of protecting people at work, and **Cities of Today, Cities of Tomorrow**, which contains six units on the history, potential, and problems of urbanization. Other units address peace, poverty, human rights, and health.

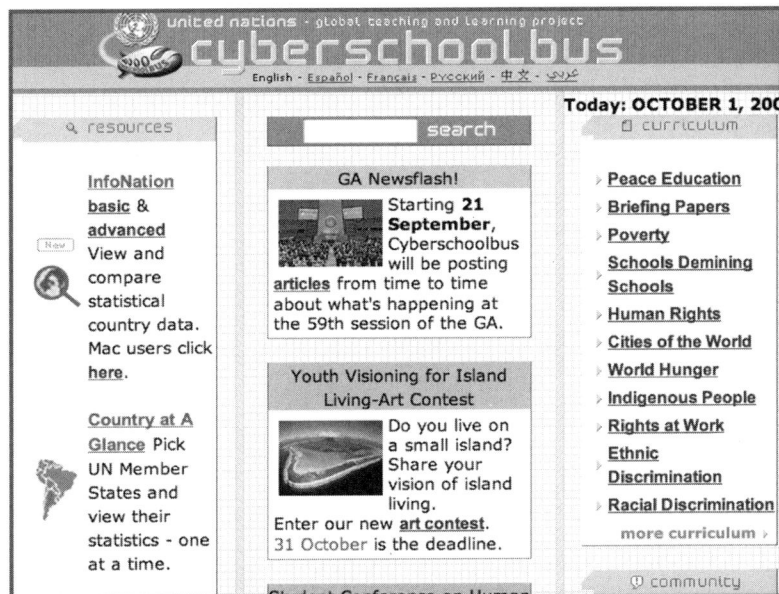

## Digital History

### www.digitalhistory.uh.edu

**SITE DESCRIPTION:** The Digital History Web site exists to support the teaching of American History in K–12 schools and colleges. It's supported by the Department of History and the College of Education at the University of Houston. The site consists of an original multimedia **Textbook**, collections of original and annotated documents, succinct essays on themes in U.S. history (such as history of film, ethnicity, private life, or technology), classroom handouts, multimedia exhibitions, chronologies, maps, audio archives (speeches and book talks), and visual archives. You can navigate the site by either using the graphics links on the home page or the list of contents on the left-hand side of most pages.

**HIGHLIGHTS FOR TEACHERS:** Digital History contains many notable features for both teachers and students. **Interactive Timeline** is very cool and unique, functioning as an interface between a timeline of U.S. history and an active map of the United States. It not only explains key events, it also shows where they took place. The **Doing History** area presents great exhibits on **Courtship**, **Decision Making**, and **Fashion**, and offers guidelines for conducting one's own historical research in 10 additional areas, such as **Advertising**, **Food**, **Graveyards**, and **Propaganda**.

The handouts are wonderful, and the 24 modules on key periods of American history contain an overview, recommended documents, films, images, and teaching resources (including lesson plans). The **Reference Room** contains an outstanding collection of links to a great many persons, places, and things historical, while **Ask the HyperHistorian** enables visitors to ask questions related to anything on the site.

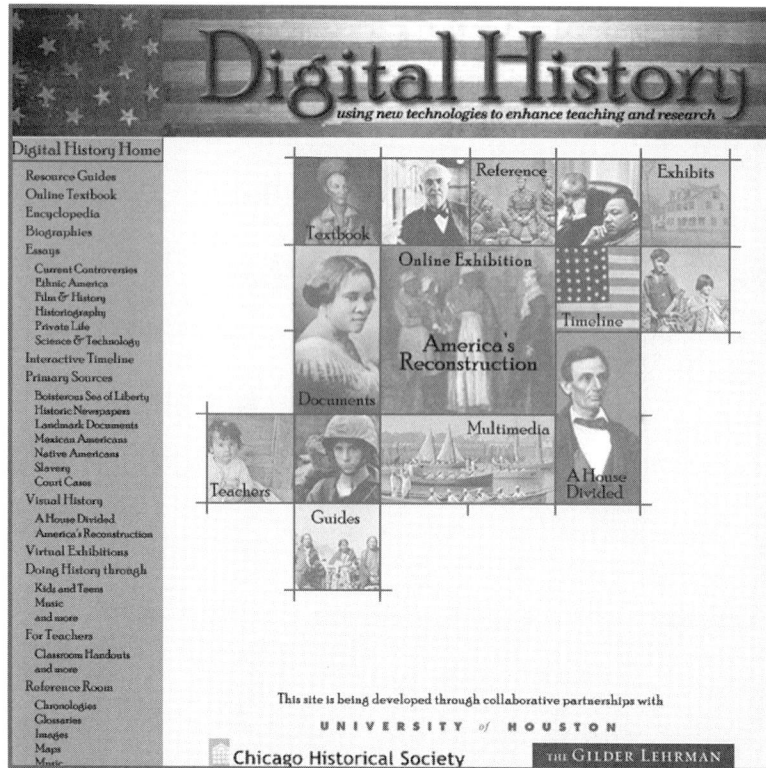

## Famous Trials

www.law.umkc.edu/faculty/projects/ftrials/ftrials.htm

**SITE DESCRIPTION:** Trials have always captivated the popular mind—and the scholar's, too. As Jon Katz (media critic and former executive producer of the *CBS Evening News*) wrote in *Wired* magazine: "Our communal and civic open spaces—courts, workplaces, Congress, academe, the media—are no longer places where issues are settled, but battlegrounds on which our most pressing conflicts will never be resolved."

Whether you agree with Katz or not, there's no doubt that every few years a trial comes along that in the most dramatic of ways seems to precipitate competing cultural forces and illuminate fundamental social conflicts.

Professor Doug Linder, author of this Web site, has created more than 50 collections of transcripts, maps, pictures, audio clips, primary documents, timelines, Web links, newspaper accounts, editorial cartoons, and his own personal essays to give visitors a penetrating view of each trial, its social and historical context, and the larger conflicts that were played out within the confines of the courtroom.

**HIGHLIGHTS FOR TEACHERS:** A sample of the trials covered includes the **Trial of Socrates**, the **Trial of Jesus**, the **Trial of Galileo**, the **Amistad Trials**, the **Johnson Impeachment**, the **Three Trials of Oscar Wilde**, the **Bill Haywood Trial**, the **Triangle Shirtwaist Fire Trial**, the **Scopes "Monkey" Trial**, the **My Lai Courts Martial**, the **Charles Manson Trial**, the **LAPD Officers' (King Beating) Trial**, and the **O. J. Simpson Trial**.

At the bottom of the home page, visitors will also find links to Professor Linder's other Web sites, including **Other Famous American Trials** and **Famous World Trials**. More personal sites by the author include the essay **Building "Famous Trials."** For fun, go to the subhead in the essay titled Enjoy the Making and click on the links to **Bill of Rights Golf**, **Constitutional Jeopardy**, and **Who Wants to Marry a Founding Father**.

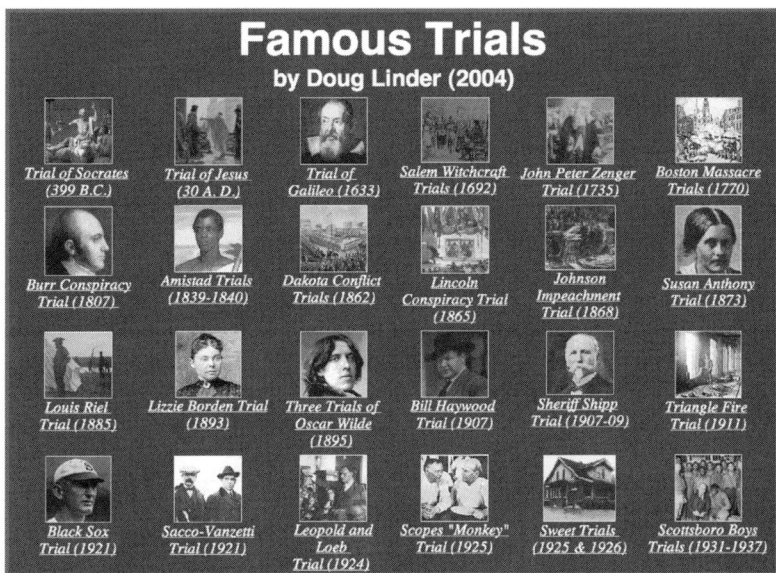

## History/Social Studies for K–12 Teachers

home.comcast.net/~dboals1/boals.html

**SITE DESCRIPTION:** Dennis Boals has created the ultimate hotlist for social studies educators. This no-frills site consists of a categorized list of links to social studies and history topics— thousands and thousands of links. Among the 28 diverse categories are **Humanities/Art**; **Resources for Parents**; **K–12 Resources**; **Research/Critical Thinking**; **Diversity**; **Kids and Students**; **Electronic Texts, Books and Zines**; **Government**; and **American History**.

When you navigate to one of the 28 categories, it's divided in turn into subcategories. For example, the **Diversity** collection (one of the best collections of diversity resources on the Web) contains **General Sources**, **The Cultural Landscape**, **Disabilities**, **Migration and Immigration Sources**, **Jewish Resources**, **Asian American**, **African American**, **Women's Studies**, **Native American**, and **Hispanic**. Each subcategory holds dozens and dozens of links. Most include brief site descriptions.

**HIGHLIGHTS FOR TEACHERS:** Each month, Mr. Boals provides an update of sites that have been added to each section in the **NEW** area. This can be a good way to browse for current resources and find some real gems.

The **Creative Applications** section is particularly rewarding to browse through. Some of the sites that can be found here include **Walks Inside Venice** (a walking tour of Venice), **Virtual Mummy** (unwrap a mummy just by clicking your mouse), and the marvelous **Tempus Fugit: Time Flies** virtual exhibit from the Nelson-Atkins Museum of Art in Kansas City.

## Humanities-Interactive

www.humanities-interactive.org/a_base_UD.html

**SITE DESCRIPTION:** This wonderful Web site hosts a growing collection of multimedia exhibits, grouped into seven categories: **Border Studies**; **Texas History, Texas Culture**; **Ancient Cultures of Our World**; **The Medieval World**; **The New World**; **Understanding Other Cultures**; and **Literature & Our Imaginative Heritage**. Each category contains anywhere from 4 to 16 exhibits, for a total of about 50. Ten more exhibits in two new categories (American History, American Culture; and The Arts and the Humanities) are promised in the near future. Exhibits consist of an online slideshow, an interpretive essay, a teaching guide, learning activities, and (in many cases) one or more interactive games.

**HIGHLIGHTS FOR TEACHERS:** These rich, museum-grade exhibits not only exist online, they're also available for rent. Schools and organizations may rent the exhibits for a three-week period at a nominal shipping cost (generally $200–$400). Through 2005, authorized nonprofit organizations in Texas may apply to the project's sponsor, Humanities Texas, for a grant to offset this cost. Exhibit titles include **Mexico: Splendors of Thirty Centuries**; **Border Studies: The Texas-Mexico Border**; **Invasion Yanqui: The Mexican War, 1846–1848**; **The Treasures of Tutankhamun**; **Pompeii, A.D. 79**; **The Legacy of the Middle East**; **Africa in the Americas**; **The Peruvians**; **Istanbul: Portrait of a City**; **The Art of Chivalry**; **The Treasury of San Marco, Venice**; and **The Shogun Age**.

A catalog, available for downloading on this site, also lists hundreds of audiovisuals (videocassettes, narrated slide shows, audiotapes, etc.) that can be rented for $10 per week.

## HyperHistory Online

**www.hyperhistory.com/online_n2/History_n2/a.html**

**SITE DESCRIPTION:** HyperHistory Online is the amazing creation of a single talented individual, Andreas Nothiger. He has attempted (with considerable success) to summarize and portray the history of the entire world from 1000 B.C.E. to the present day. This project was made possible by the rise of the Internet and the evolution of hypertext, and Mr. Nothiger makes use of these tools in creative and meaningful ways.

It's almost too formidable a task to even conceive of: channeling, into one meaningful stream, the turbulent flow of world events, ideas, cultures, politics, and technologies spanning 3,000 years. Mr. Nothiger has accomplished this by creating a unique system of representation that involves color-coded charts and maps, along with hyperlinks to Web sites and materials both on and off his own site.

**HIGHLIGHTS FOR TEACHERS:** Visitors to the site may not always agree with either the choices Mr. Nothiger has made or the events and people he has emphasized. Nevertheless, HyperHistory Online does capture a tremendous amount of information, and it synthesizes it in ways that permit readers to see relationships, progressions, and historical threads they may not have been able to grasp before. The maps and concurrent timelines are artfully rendered, and the links throughout the site work swiftly and accurately. HyperHistory Online has been commended by a number of well-known organizations, including Encyclopedia Britannica, the History Channel, and Discovery Channel School.

As with any work as original and ambitious as this one, HyperHistory Online requires visitors to put forth considerable effort to get the most they can out of the site. There's no user's guide, so you must invest time and energy learning how to read the charts and access the on- and off-site resources. The payoff, however, is likely to be quite satisfactory.

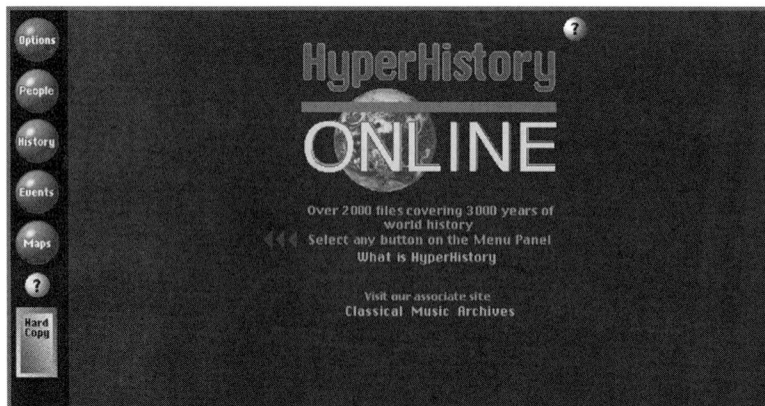

# iEARN

**www.iearn.org**

**SITE DESCRIPTION:** Student visitors to iEARN are encouraged to participate in collaborative, online educational projects that can make a difference in the world. These projects represent a great way for young people to engage in responsible social activism and grow in their knowledge of important issues confronting the world community.

More than 160 **Projects** are listed on the iEARN site, grouped into categories such as **Creative/ Language Arts**, **Science/Environment/Math**, **Social Studies**, and **Learning Circles**. Information is available in 30 different languages, reflecting the true worldwide reach of this site. More than 15,000 schools from 100 countries belong to the iEARN network. On any given day, as many as 1 million students are involved in collaborative projects through iEARN.

If you find the home page difficult to navigate, click on the **Site Map** at the top of the page. This takes you to a well-organized list of all the sections of iEARN.

**HIGHLIGHTS FOR TEACHERS:** Teachers can select a specific project that fits their curriculum, classroom needs, and schedules. Once a project is picked, the class may enter an online space to become part of a collaborative effort with other classes from around the world. Participation in projects helps students improve their research and critical-thinking skills, while allowing them to experience technology as a tool to get things done. Finally, taking part raises students' cultural awareness and encourages them to become involved in community issues.

## Internet History Sourcebooks Project
**www.fordham.edu/halsall/**

**SITE DESCRIPTION:** This excellent Web site offers direct access to significant historical documents and primary sources, many of which can only be found here. The sources are well organized and fully searchable, so visitors can find what they're looking for with relative ease. The site also contains extensive pages (many of which include full lecture notes) for courses taught by site developer Paul Halsall, a professor at Fordham University. Topics include Western civilization, European history, modern history, medieval Europe, Byzantine history, the Crusades, sex and gender in premodern Europe, saints, sainthood and society, and Chinese studies.

The Internet history sourcebooks are collections of public domain and copy-permitted historical texts for educational use. The three main sourcebooks focus on **Ancient History**, **Medieval History**, and **Modern History**. Subsidiary sourcebooks are organized around the following areas of history: **African**, **East Asian**, **Indian**, **Islamic**, **Global**, **Jewish**, **Lesbian and Gay**, **Science**, and **Women's**.

**HIGHLIGHTS FOR TEACHERS:** This site has gained a well-earned reputation as the single best place to go on the Web for access to primary and original sources (as well as to meticulously selected secondary sources) in the many areas of history indicated above. Professor Halsall maintains a separate set of resources on **Ancient Law** and **Medieval Law**. Teachers will enjoy comparing the course pages with their own syllabi. Two areas of the site are especially enjoyable: the professor's extensive examination of, and references to, feature and documentary films, and his collection on **Medieval NYC** (New York City).

## The Learning Page . . . Especially for Teachers

lcweb2.loc.gov/learn/

**SITE DESCRIPTION:** The Learning Page is a teacher's guide to the **American Memory** collections of the Library of Congress, the largest library in the world. **American Memory** is "an online archive of more than 100 collections of rare and unique items important to America's heritage. The collections contain more than 7 million primary source documents, photographs, films, and recordings that reflect the collective American memory."

The Learning Page is organized into six sections: **Getting Started**, **Lesson Plans**, **Features & Activities**, **Collection Connections**, **Community Center**, and **Professional Development**. **Features & Activities** has 19 interactive puzzles, games, and collaborative projects that address such topics as food, holidays, flight, copyright, and immigration. **Port of Entry** and **Historical Detective** are extensive multimedia units with exceptionally rich graphic materials and information. They focus on honing students' research skills.

**HIGHLIGHTS FOR TEACHERS:** **Lesson Plans** are organized in two ways: (1) by **Theme**, **Topic**, **Discipline**, or **Era**, and (2) by **Title**. Specific grade levels are indicated for each lesson; most cover Grades 4 and up and are multiday units rather than single lessons. The organization and quality of plans are excellent; rich in graphics and original sources, they often come with separate areas for teachers and students.

Be sure to look at **Self-Serve** workshops under **Professional Development**. These can be used for self-study, in teachers' study groups, or even as instructional resources for students. Areas include Classroom Applications, Search Skills, Technology, and Working with Primary Sources. Don't miss the link to **The Source** at the bottom of the home page. *The Source* is an e-zine that contains practical teaching tips for those who use **American Memory**.

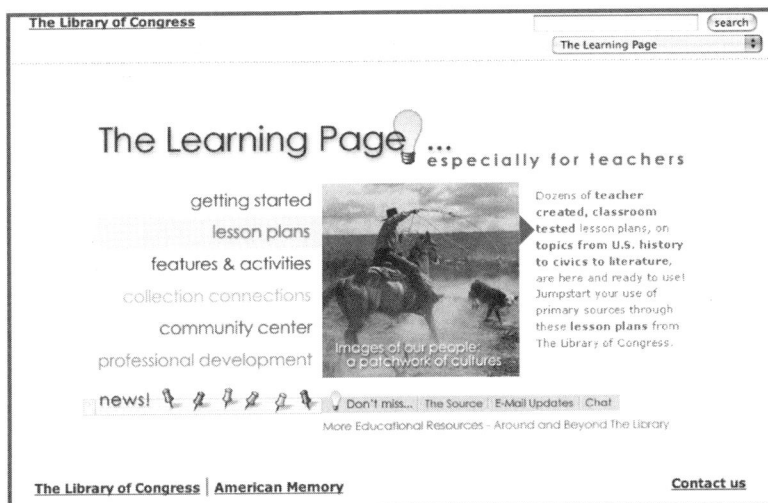

## National Geographic Education Guide
**www.nationalgeographic.com/education/**

**SITE DESCRIPTION:** This is the terrific National Geographic Web site's home base for teachers. It's organized to show National Geographic's collection of education sites, with tabs linking to **Lesson Plans**, **Maps & Photos**, **Professional Development**, and **Current Events**.

The home page contains two useful search engines. At the center of the page is the one-stop supersearch, where users enter keywords. Results from the National Geographic database are organized by type: Maps, Photos and Art, Articles and Information, Games and Features, and Audio and Video. The second search engine is called Find Resources. Users enter a subject, resource type, and grade.

Visitors can also find home page links to other areas of the larger National Geographic site. They are organized in categories that include Educator Favorites, More Guides, and More from National Geographic, which features online versions of all four of the organization's magazines: *National Geographic, National Geographic Kids, National Geographic Traveler,* and *National Geographic Adventure.*

**HIGHLIGHTS FOR TEACHERS:** Here's an insider's clue: click on the **Site Index** in the black toolbar at the bottom of the home page, then select **Education**. Because the home page is crowded, using this link makes it easier to find what you're looking for. The **Education** link also provides access to additional useful material, including National Geographic's great Activities and Games, the wonderful Xpeditions site (mentioned in chapter 4 under MarcoPolo), and Geography Resources.

The **Maps and Geography** resources are also outstanding. The **MapMachine** enables visitors to find nearly any place on Earth and view it by population, climate, and much more. The Xpeditions Atlas has hundreds of outline maps for school use, a star chart atlas of the night sky, and excellent conservation maps.

# Newsweek Education Program
www.newsweekeducation.com

**SITE DESCRIPTION:** This program's keystone is the weekly teachers' guide, called Newsweek ThisWeek. Interested teachers may access Newsweek ThisWeek online for free every week, or if your school purchases a classroom subscription to *Newsweek,* Newsweek ThisWeek will be sent to you along with the magazine. Each issue of the guide connects questions and activities to the National Council for Social Studies theme standards. It contains **Grasping Graphics**, to help students analyze news graphics. The guide further includes a **Focus on Writing**, **Tooning In** (interpretation of editorial cartoons), and **Words and Terms in the News** (vocabulary development). Newsweek ThisWeek guides are archived back to 2000, and the search function enables visitors to scan them quickly for needed information.

The Newsweek Education Program home page provides one-click access to additional teaching resources and to *Newsweek's* secret weapon, its on-call professional staff. Five accomplished professionals are available through e-mail or a toll-free phone call to answer questions, make suggestions, and lend support in such areas as curriculum and professional development, making the best use of the Newsweek Education Program, or having a *Newsweek* presence "at your next meeting or conference."

**HIGHLIGHTS FOR TEACHERS:** While subscribers get better goodies, the Web site offers plenty to support good teaching and learning. By clicking on **Resources** in the black toolbar near the top of the page, visitors may select from **NewsSources**, **Skills Builders**, **Issues Today Maps**, **Curriculum Guides**, **Making the Most of Newsweek ThisWeek**, "**My Turn**," and **Extras!** Sample activities are available online for each of these resources, but again, you must be a subscriber to get the complete hard-copy versions. However, don't hesitate to contact your regional manager for help, regardless of whether you subscribe—you'll be pleasantly surprised at how helpful they will be.

# SCORE: History/Social Science

score.rims.k12.ca.us

**SITE DESCRIPTION:** SCORE stands for Schools of California Online Resources for Education. It was originally funded in the late 1990s by the California Department of Education. It's now funded and managed by the California Technology Assistance Project.

In addition to its history and social science page, SCORE has three other areas for the disciplines of mathematics, science, and language arts. Although SCORE discusses California's standards and statewide curriculum, visitors will find outstanding resources and activities applicable to any school's curriculum. SCORE comes with an online tutorial, and all SCORE resources have been created, validated, and organized by practicing California educators.

The home page consists of two sets of links. The list on the left consists mainly of general information about the background and history of SCORE; the areas titled **Internet Classrooms** and **Teacher Talk** offer useful information. At the bottom of the column is a place to subscribe to SCORE's e-mail newsletter.

**HIGHLIGHTS FOR TEACHERS:** The Find Online Resources section is first-rate. Visitors may begin with **Find Resources & Lessons by Grade Level**. Each grade has a theme, within which are numerous units that contain both resources and activities. Visitors can also return to the home page and **Find Resources & Lessons by Topic/Keyword**.

## Special Projects: Understanding World Events
www.esrnational.org/sp/we/world.htm

**SITE DESCRIPTION:** This Web site is maintained by Educators for Social Responsibility, a national nonprofit organization founded in 1982. Its mission is "to make teaching social responsibility a core practice in education." This particular page focuses on helping young people cope with, and better understand, global issues and crisis events. It consists of teaching resources, lessons, guides, sponsored events, and lists of best-of-Web links.

Topics addressed include **Current Events Lessons**, **Dealing with Crises**, **Understanding War**, **Countering Discrimination**, and **Analyzing 9/11**. Among the **Current Events Lessons** presently listed on the site are USA Patriot Act—Security vs. Privacy, and Human Rights, Human Wrongs. Notable items in the **Understanding War** section include lessons on security and conflict, the **Believing Game**, the **Doubting Game**, **Understanding Propaganda**, and role-playing activities dealing with policy options in Iraq.

**HIGHLIGHTS FOR TEACHERS:** Under **Countering Discrimination**, specific lessons may be found discussing how to deal with stereotyping, prejudice, discrimination, and scapegoating. At the bottom of this page is a link to the Educational Development Center's series of lessons titled **Beyond Blame: Reacting to the Terrorist Attack**. Resources for dealing with September 11 and its aftermath include lessons on **Understanding Afghanistan** and **Responding to Violent Events by Building Community: Action Ideas for Students and Schools**.

The site also offers a free monthly e-newsletter. Click on **About Us**, then select the link **monthly e-newsletter**.

# CHAPTER 9

# Technology Integration

The Web sites in this chapter are full of great ideas for infusing technology into the secondary classroom. Best Practices of Technology Integration offers more than 1,000 lessons that integrate technology with core content. Edutopia presents articles, tutorials, professional development modules, and more than 70 videos of exemplary classroom practices, while techLEARNING.com: Technology & Learning provides a gold mine of how-tos, best practices, topical articles, and teaching tips. InTime catalogs more than 600 video vignettes of PK–12 teachers working to integrate technology with all subject areas.

Along similar lines, Internet4Classrooms furnishes many software tutorials and a superb list of both curriculum and professional Web sites for teachers. BioPoint's Course Productivity WebTools offers numerous tools for teaching, including templates to create your own Web site without having to use HTML and a tool for downloading entire Web sites to your computer. Also providing numerous valuable tools is the High Plains Regional Technology in Education Consortium. Finally, Nicenet Internet Classroom Assistant provides a free online space (with no advertising) to hold private threaded discussions and share documents, links, and personal messages.

# QUICK REFERENCE CHART

| Technology Integration | FEATURES FOR TEACHERS | | | | | | |
|---|---|---|---|---|---|---|---|
| Name of Site/URL | chat or forum | lesson plans | teacher resources | parent resources | teacher's guide | video, audio, applets | Web links |
| **Best Practices of Technology Integration** www.remc11.k12.mi.us/bstpract | | | | | | | |
| **Biopoint's Course Productivity WebTools** www.biopoint.com/webtools/ coursetools.html | | | | | | | |
| **Edutopia (George Lucas Educational Foundation)** www.glef.org | | | | | | | |
| **High Plains Regional Technology in Education Consortium** www.hprtec.org | | | | | | | |
| **Internet4Classrooms** www.internet4classrooms.com | | | | | | | |
| **InTime** www.intime.uni.edu | | | | | | | |
| **Nicenet Internet Classroom Assistant** www.nicenet.org | | | | | | | |
| **techLEARNING.com: Technology & Learning** www.techlearning.com | | | | | | | |

The shaded boxes indicate the feature is available on the Web site.

# QUICK REFERENCE CHART *(continued)*

| Technology Integration | FEATURES FOR TEACHERS | | | FEATURES FOR STUDENTS | | |
|---|---|---|---|---|---|---|
| Name of Site/URL | assessment ideas | e-newsletter | reproducibles | activities | interactive exercises | reading material |
| **Best Practices of Technology Integration** www.remc11.k12.mi.us/bstpract | ■ | | | | | |
| **Biopoint's Course Productivity WebTools** www.biopoint.com/webtools/ coursetools.html | | | | ■ | ■ | ■ |
| **Edutopia (George Lucas Educational Foundation)** www.glef.org | ■ | *Edutopia News* | | ■ | ■ | ■ |
| **High Plains Regional Technology in Education Consortium** www.hprtec.org | ■ | | ■ | ■ | ■ | ■ |
| **Internet4Classrooms** www.internet4classrooms.com | ■ | | ■ | ■ | ■ | ■ |
| **InTime** www.intime.uni.edu | ■ | | | ■ | ■ | ■ |
| **Nicenet Internet Classroom Assistant** www.nicenet.org | | | | | ■ | |
| **techLEARNING.com: Technology & Learning** www.techlearning.com | ■ | *TechLearning News* | | | | |

The shaded boxes indicate the feature is available on the Web site.

## Best Practices of Technology Integration
www.remc11.k12.mi.us/bstpract

**SITE DESCRIPTION:** This Web site has gathered more than 1,000 lessons—submitted by teachers from throughout the state of Michigan—that integrate technology with core content. All grade levels and subject areas are addressed, and the site is conveniently organized into elementary, middle, and high school grade bands. A team of educators has classroom-tested and evaluated all lessons for inclusion on the site.

Despite the fact that this site was first published in 1998, the lessons remain fresh and applicable today. All lesson plans come with complete descriptions that enable teachers to replicate or modify them, and all correlate with Michigan state standards. What's interesting about these technology integration ideas is that only a few short years ago they were considered cutting edge. Today, many of these technology and presentation tools are competently used by students much younger than the original target participants.

**HIGHLIGHTS FOR TEACHERS:** As almost any educator with experience using technology would expect, most of these lessons are interdisciplinary and project-based. Some of the best lesson plans include **Internet Research Assistant** (under High School **Integrated Arts**); **Twenty-two points, plus triple-word-score, plus fifty points for using all my letters. Game's over. I'm outta here** (under High School **Integrated Arts**); and **Statistical Pictures of School and Life** (under High School **Mathematics**).

Welcome to the Best Practices of Technology Integration in Michigan Site. This site is sponsored by the Michigan Association of Intermediate School Administrators, the REMC Association of Michigan, and the Great Lakes Educational Network (Glen). The lesson plans that you will find here have been written by practicing teachers and have been "kid tested" to work in the classroom. All of these lessons have been aligned with the Michigan Framework Document. We hope you find these lessons helpful. They are examples of how technology can be used as a valuable tool in your classroom. Please feel free to try or adapt any of these lessons in your classroom

This Project has received funding from the Michigan Technology Literacy Challenge Grant Fund, the Michigan Department of Education, the REMC Association of Michigan, and the Berrien County Intermediate School District.

| Elementary | Middle School | High School |
|---|---|---|
| Fine Arts Integrated Arts Language Arts Mathematics Science Social Studies | Fine Arts Integrated Arts Language Arts Mathematics Science Social Studies | Business Fine Arts Integrated Arts Language Arts Mathematics Science Social Studies |

## Biopoint's Course Productivity WebTools
www.biopoint.com/webtools/coursetools.html

**SITE DESCRIPTION:** Here's a no-nonsense spot that gives educators easy access to a suite of online tools to enhance personal efficiency. Want to create an online presence but don't have the time to learn HTML? Biopoint has a link to a place on the Web with a free Web page template all set up for you (**myprojectpages.com**). Want to build your own rubrics or see what others have created? **Rubric Builder** and **Rubistar** are links to sites that do just that.

**HIGHLIGHTS FOR TEACHERS:** What's great about this site is that it's gathered so many practical and useful online tools in one place. Go to **QuizCenter** to develop your own online quizzes that will score themselves automatically and report those scores to you immediately, all for free. Go to **Hot Potatoes** to create interactive multiple-choice, short-answer, jumbled-sentence, crossword, matching, or fill-in-the-blank exercises—also for free. Check out **WebZip**, a program that enables you to download entire Web pages to your computer for offline viewing. This is great for the classroom having only one or two wired computers. **Nicenet** gives you free online space to conference with your students, post assignments, and even collect homework.

## Edutopia (George Lucas Educational Foundation)
**www.glef.org**

**SITE DESCRIPTION:** The folks at the George Lucas Educational Foundation (GLEF) believe passionately in the power of technology to transform education for all stakeholders. This Web site provides concrete evidence that this is happening all across the nation and gives educators specific guidance regarding how they can be a part of this transformation. As you might expect, the site is graphically quite advanced, employing lots of video. The site shares a name with the foundation's new print magazine *Edutopia*; follow the link at the top of the page to obtain a free subscription.

The GLEF site is thoughtfully organized. Arrayed across the top of the home page are five small boxes that take visitors to a description of the **Magazine**, **Documentaries**, **Multimedia**, **Professional Development**, and the GLEF **Store**. Down the left side of the page are five categories of interest: Get Started, About Us, Free Subscriptions, Topics (including **Assessment**, **Digital Divide**, **Technology Integration**), and the Internet Radio Show. This last item is an interesting collection of weekly, one-hour Webcasts of interviews with leading educators, students, and education policy makers, moderated by GLEF Executive Director Milton Chen.

**HIGHLIGHTS FOR TEACHERS:** Don't miss the invaluable sections **Ongoing Professional Development** and **Technology Professional Development**, in the Topics area. **Technology Integration** takes you to a set of linked pages set up like a magazine, with a feature article, a section titled What's Working for K–12 Schools, Watch & Learn, a featured interview with a teacher or other education expert, an online Courseware Module on technology integration, and access to the Big List—GLEF's entire library on the subject of technology integration. Here, visitors can access a complete archive of articles, courseware modules, and multimedia.

## High Plains Regional Technology in Education Consortium
www.hprtec.org

**SITE DESCRIPTION:** The tools offered by the High Plains Regional Technology in Education Consortium (HPR*TEC) look simple when laid out neatly on this Web page. They are, in fact, simple to use, but the results they produce are profound. Each one can help you or your students to work more efficiently and effectively. HPR*TEC is a University of Kansas program funded by the U.S. Department of Education. Everything here is free.

**HIGHLIGHTS FOR TEACHERS:** Here's a brief summary of each of the tools. **Action Research Network** provides a template for teachers to use to post their research or view the work of others. **Assign-A-Day** enables teachers to produce, for students' online viewing, a class calendar and assignments. Teachers can use **Casa Notes**' templates to send parents quick, run-of-the-mill notes in either Spanish or English. **Edlines** are headlines from, and links to, education stories that come from media outlets around the nation. **Kids' Vid** helps students and teachers use video production to support project-based learning. **Learning Associates Network** provides inservice materials to educators who teach others how to use the HPR*TEC tools. **NoteStar** enables students to take notes from online sources and maintain them online, with citation information entered automatically. **PRISM: Polar Explorer** provides real-time data to students and teachers regarding a University of Kansas project that involves expeditions to Greenland and Antarctica. **ProfilerPRO** users can create, administer, and interpret online surveys. **R*TEC Teachers** enables users to select a subject and conduct a search for related WebQuests, Tracks, and ThinkQuests. **Think Tank** helps students develop topics for reports. The most popular tool is **RubiStar**. With it, teachers can easily develop, online, their own custom rubrics, or they can use examples developed by others. Using **QuizStar** teachers can "create a custom quiz that learners can take online." **TrackStar** offers a template to create HPR*TEC's version of a WebQuest; users may create their own or use Tracks developed by others. The tool **PBL Checklists** enables you to develop custom checklists in both Spanish and English to guide students through projects. Finally, the **Web Worksheet Wizard** walks you through steps to make a worksheet, lesson, or page to post online, all without having to use any difficult codes.

# HPR★TEC
High Plains Regional Technology in Education Consortium

**A network of solutions**

"NoteStar is the newest utility to assist Project Based Learning on the World Wide Web. Designed for 4th thru 12th grade students, NoteStar assists in taking notes from online sources. Using the NoteStar NoteCards tool, students can take notes from online sources as they browse the Internet. Source information (i.e. title, url, etc.) is automatically captured in order to assist in work

Action Research Network
Assign-A-Day
Casa Notes
Edlines
Kids' Vid
Learning Associates Network
NoteStar
PRISM: Polar Explorer
PBL Checklists
ProfilerPRO
QuizStar
R*TEC Teachers
RubiStar
Tech Topics
Think Tank
TrackStar
Web Worksheet Wizard

## Internet4Classrooms

**www.internet4classrooms.com**

**SITE DESCRIPTION:** Of all the great Web sites in this chapter, Internet4Classrooms is clearly the best for just-in-time teacher technology help. This site compiles a huge array of useful curricula and professional Web sites, specific tutorials for the classroom's most commonly used computer applications, links to the top online education news publications, links to grant information, a guide to searching the Web, templates for planning Web-based lessons, and a slightly modified version of a WebQuest, called WebGuide.

Internet4Classrooms is the brainchild of Susan Brooks and Bill Byles, technology and professional development specialists from the Memphis City Schools in Tennessee. This site has logged more than 3.5 million visitors since November 2000.

**HIGHLIGHTS FOR TEACHERS: Links for K–12 Teachers** consists of three categories: Subjects, Interests, and Assessment. Hundreds of sites are listed both alphabetically and by grade level; most are described briefly. Topics and themes of interest to teachers—**Computers**, **Graphics & Multimedia**, **Idea Starters**, **Lesson Plans**, **Project Ideas**, **Teacher Tools**, and **Virtual Field Trips**—are explored in the Interests category, while specific skill reinforcement exercises and sample state tests for Grades K–8 can be found in the Assessment section.

**Daily Dose of the Web** provides links to more than 100 sites offering daily questions and activities for teachers and students. They're grouped by **Question of the Day**, **Subject Area**, **Quotation Sources**, **Brain Teasers**, and **Interesting Trivia**. **Ed News** provides links to eight top online education publications, including *Education Week, Instructor, T.H.E. Journal, Technology and Learning,* and *U.S. DOE News.* Grant information is compiled from 16 different sources. The **Modules** section features 15 user-friendly tutorials for such applications as PowerPoint, Word, Excel, Inspiration, Internet Explorer, Dreamweaver, and HyperStudio. It also provides links to more than two-dozen additional tutorials for these and other applications, for both the Mac and PC platforms.

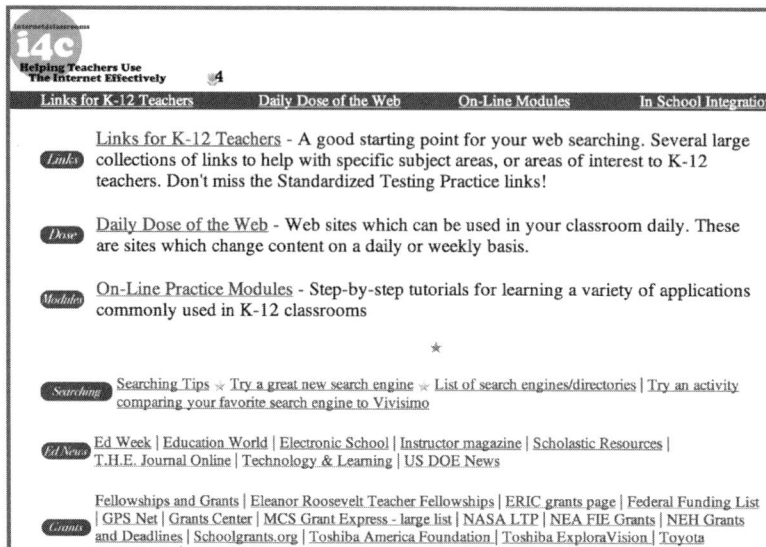

# InTime

**www.intime.uni.edu**

**SITE DESCRIPTION:** InTime is a great way to get ideas for infusing good technology practices into your classroom. The site is a compilation of "video vignettes of PK–12 teachers from various grades and subjects [who] integrate technology into their classrooms using numerous teaching strategies." Nearly 600 video vignettes have been compiled, catalogued, and carefully analyzed so that viewers can search by grade level, content area, and elements of the teaching model used. Lesson plans for the videos and written transcripts are also provided. Substantial portions of the written material on InTime, including simultaneous written transcripts of the videos, are available in Spanish, Portuguese, French, Kiswahili, Romanian, Russian, and Chinese. This project is funded by the U.S. Department of Education.

**HIGHLIGHTS FOR TEACHERS:** The videos of actual teachers using technology in the classroom are fascinating to watch and very educational. The in-depth analysis that each lesson is subjected to can help teachers reflect on the many instructional decisions they make every day: why certain decisions are made, what factors influence decisions one way or another, what consequences result from decisions in terms of student learning and other outcomes, how time and resources are managed in the classroom, and optimal ways to sequence and structure a lesson, to name just a few.

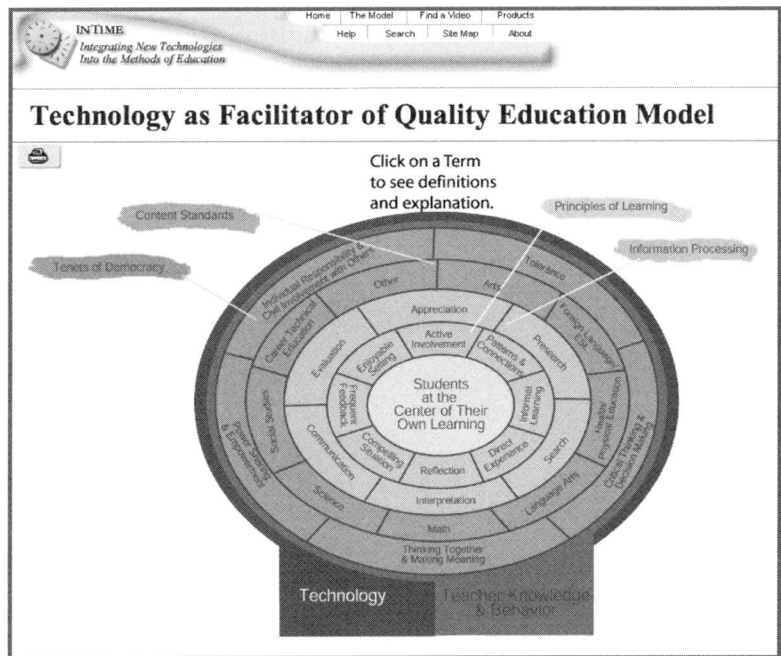

## Nicenet Internet Classroom Assistant

www.nicenet.org

**SITE DESCRIPTION:** The Web site that eventually became Internet Classroom Assistant (ICA) came online in 1995. In Internet time, that was a millennium ago, as reflected in the site's current statement of philosophy:

> Before the commercial frenzy of the "dot com" years, the Internet was home to a thriving culture of openness and sharing. This culture was born from the distributed, peer-to-peer nature of the Net, a model that to this day stands in stark contrast to the one-to-many print and broadcast commercial mass media. Nicenet's foundation was built upon this spirit of free-flowing ideas and new possibilities.

> The ICA was first conceived as a Web-based classroom environment that could be used by post-secondary teachers with their students. The system was designed not as a replacement for the classroom, but rather as a supplement allowing greater communication and sharing of information among students and between teachers and their students. However, Nicenet does not restrict the use of the ICA for any purpose and our users have frequently found creative and unimagined uses for the ICA.

**HIGHLIGHTS FOR TEACHERS:** So, what does the site do? It enables anyone to set up an online "classroom" where users can conference (conduct a private, threaded discussion), schedule (put a schedule online), share documents (publish documents, turn in papers, and give classmates peer-to-peer feedback), use personal messaging (like Instant Messaging, but way before AOL did it), and share links.

The resources on the site are free and work with any browser. A few years ago, numerous free sites tried to create this kind of online collaborative environment. Now, they're almost completely gone, or charge a monthly fee. ICA was the first, and it may outlast them all.

## techLEARNING.com: Technology & Learning

**www.techlearning.com**

**SITE DESCRIPTION:** *Technology and Learning* is one of the most respected print periodicals devoted to educational technology. It's for teachers at all levels. This Web site archives back issues of the magazine and provides additional online-only resources. On techLEARNING.com, visitors will find a gold mine of how-tos, best practices, topical articles, grant and contest information, and professional development support.

The Web site is organized in two ways. The first is by job function, listed in a toolbar across the top: **Teachers**, **Technology Coordinators**, and **Administrators**. The second is by interest area, listed in a box down the left-hand side of the home page: **T&L Magazine**, **Educators' Outlook**, **DV** (digital video) **in the Classroom**, **School CIO**, **Resources**, **T&L Events**, and **Free Newsletters**.

**HIGHLIGHTS FOR TEACHERS:** A number of areas in techLEARNING.com will be particularly interesting and useful to teachers: under **T&L Magazine**, click on **Departments** and look at the list of **Feature** articles; be sure to check out the **How-To:** list of tips and tricks; and you'll want to discover **What Works** for best practices. Under **Educators' Outlook**, **Articles From the Classroom** provide many creative and practical ideas, while **Sites for Educators** supplies numerous articles and descriptions of Web sites grouped by subject discipline.

Under **Resources**, don't miss **Grants Database**, **PDQ** (Professional Development Quick) tips and archive, **The IT Guy** and archive, Web Picks (a list of reader-nominated Web sites), and Web Links (to top sites organized into **Curriculum Resources**, **Research Tools**, **Resources for Planning/Administration**, **Sites for Students**, and **School Web Sites**).

# CHAPTER 10

# World Languages

**A**ccording to the American Council on the Teaching of Foreign Languages, more than 85% of American secondary students are enrolled in either Spanish or French. One of the best Internet sources for teachers of both languages is Casa de Joanna: Language Learning Resources, with its host of cultural and linguistic resources and its collection of authentic links to native-language sites. This site offers contemporary resource material and language that secondary students can relate to: Spanish clothing stores, French restaurants, European amusement parks, e-zines, supermarkets, cartoons, and online games.

BBC Languages is amazingly complete. It contains video, audio, phrases, pictures, online courses, e-zines, news broadcasts, and lesson plans for language instruction in French, Spanish, German, Italian, Greek, Portuguese, Gaelic, Welsh, Irish, Chinese, and Japanese. iLoveLanguages furnishes Web links for 209 languages, including Esperanto and Klingon (is there an Advanced Placement exam for Klingon?). Language Links catalogues teacher support sites for more than seven languages, as well as a great collection of teaching strategies.

More people speak Chinese (of one dialect or another) than any other language in the world. Absolutely the best single English language Web site about teaching Chinese is Marjorie Chan's China Links. It contains more than 600 meticulously selected and carefully described links to resources for teaching Chinese language and linguistics, as well as Chinese culture.

# QUICK REFERENCE CHART

| World Languages | FEATURES FOR TEACHERS | | | | | | |
|---|---|---|---|---|---|---|---|
| Name of Site/URL | chat or forum | lesson plans | teacher resources | parent resources | teacher's guide | video, audio, applets | Web links |
| **BBC Languages**<br>www.bbc.co.uk/languages | | | | | | | |
| **Case de Joanna:**<br>**Language Learning Resources**<br>www.casadejoanna.com | | | | | | | |
| **iLoveLanguages**<br>www.ilovelanguages.com | | | | | | | |
| **Language Links**<br>www.langlink.net | | | | | | | |
| **Marjorie Chan's China Links**<br>chinalinks.osu.edu | | | | | | | |

The shaded boxes indicate the feature is available on the Web site.

# QUICK REFERENCE CHART *(continued)*

| World Languages | FEATURES FOR TEACHERS | | | FEATURES FOR STUDENTS | | |
|---|---|---|---|---|---|---|
| **Name of Site/URL** | assessment ideas | e-newsletter | reproducibles | activities | interactive exercises | reading material |
| **BBC Languages** www.bbc.co.uk/languages | | | | | | |
| **Case de Joanna: Language Learning Resources** www.casadejoanna.com | | | | | | |
| **iLoveLanguages** www.ilovelanguages.com | | | | | | |
| **Language Links** www.langlink.net | | | | | | |
| **Marjorie Chan's China Links** chinalinks.osu.edu | | | | | | |

The shaded boxes indicate the feature is available on the Web site.

## BBC Languages

**www.bbc.co.uk/languages**

**SITE DESCRIPTION:** The extensive video and audio resources that supplement the lessons on this site make these lessons entertaining as well as useful. Most material is for beginners, but there's plenty for intermediate-level learners too. A variety of courses are offered in French, Spanish, German, Italian, Greek, Portuguese, Gaelic, Welsh, Irish, Chinese and Japanese.

Each language has its own home page, and most offer an assortment of resources, such as Courses, News and Features, For the Family, For Tutors, Phrases, For Work, For Schools, Travel, and Games and Quizzes. For teachers and students of French and Spanish, BBC Languages also produces an audio magazine.

**HIGHLIGHTS FOR TEACHERS:** Many of the lessons on the site consist of a series of short segments, just a few minutes in length. These can be easily integrated to add diversity to a language class. Click on **Staff Room** (near the bottom of the home page for each language) to access extensive resources for teachers.

On the Spanish home page, click on **BBC Mundo** to go to a full-featured Spanish-language portal site full of words and pictures, or click on **Listen** to hear a 24-hour radio broadcast in Spanish. From the French home page, click on **BBC Afrique** to access material primarily focused on the French-speaking nations of Africa. While here, visit the fascinating virtual exhibition titled The Story of Africa. It contains written material as well as an archive of 24 half-hour radio broadcasts (in English) that tell Africa's story from the dawn of humanity to the era of independence.

## Case de Joanna: Language Learning Resources

**www.casadejoanna.com**

**SITE DESCRIPTION:** Joanna Porvin has created a great spot for teachers of Spanish and French. She's collected the best Web sites and online resources for middle and high school Spanish and French teachers and brought them all together in one easy-to-navigate place. Her list of resources is deliberately brief, but users can be sure they won't be wasting their time when visiting one of Ms. Porvin's links. The main sections of the site are **Art Resources**, **French Resources**, **General Language Resources**, **Spanish Resources**, and **Teacher's Lounge**. New visitors are encouraged to make their first two stops **Casa Favorites** and the **Teacher's Lounge**.

**HIGHLIGHTS FOR TEACHERS:** The key focus of this site are what Ms. Porvin calls "authentic links" to resources for learning Spanish or French (under **Casa Favorites**). These authentic links provide good primary source material, rather than information about teaching language. Examples of authentic links include clothing store sites, sports news, restaurants, amusement parks, e-zines, museums, supermarkets, cartoons, and online games—all of which target native speakers. These authentic links have been selected with great care.

One particularly notable site highlighted here is the Latin American Resource Center at Tulane University, which has a lending library of books, kits, videos, and manipulatives that are loaned for free (borrowers pay only for return postage).

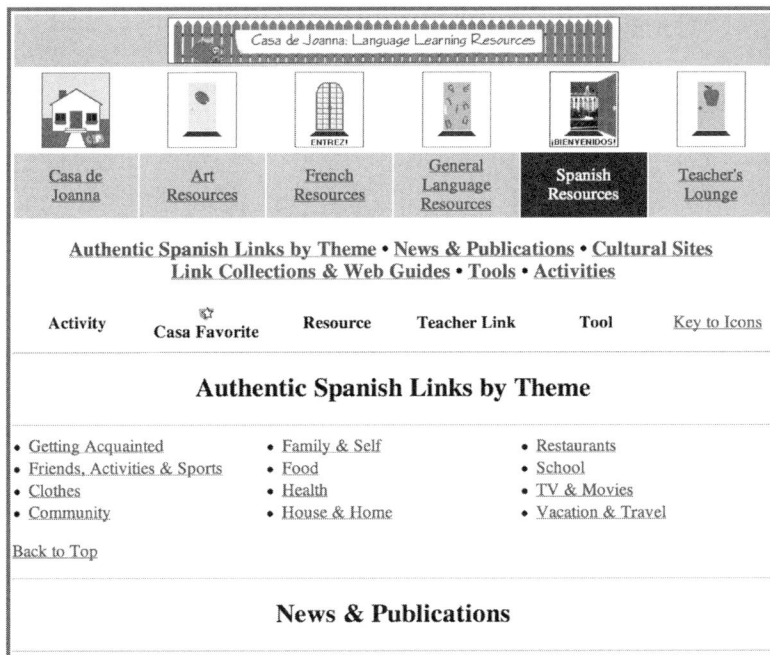

## iLoveLanguages

**www.ilovelanguages.com**

**SITE DESCRIPTION:** Since 1994, Tyler Chambers has been monitoring Web sites that support the learning of language. He has culled more than 2,000 sites, which he organizes very simply into four main categories on iLoveLanguages: **Languages**, **Schools**, **Commercial**, and **Jobs**.

**HIGHLIGHTS FOR TEACHERS:** The most useful section for secondary teachers will likely be **Languages**. This section is subdivided into 10 categories, and the list **By Language** is the most impressive. It contains 209 subcategories, from Akha to Zarma, including Esperanto and Klingon. For each language listed, visitors will find numerous helpful links.

A nice selection of **Free Translation** sites is also included under **Languages**. Computerized translation still has a long way to go, but these spots offer a valuable service—and you can't beat the price. More than 70 sites on **Linguistics** are listed.

The **Jobs** section (click on the tab at the top of the home page) will be particularly helpful to those seeking a position in a non-English-speaking country.

## Language Links

**www.langlink.net**

**polyglot.lss.wisc.edu/lss/lang/langlink.html**

**SITE DESCRIPTION:** Language Links, put together by Lauren Rosen at the University of Wisconsin, lists a multitude of sites that support teaching and learning language. Links to specific languages are located in one area of the site under such categories as **Spanish**, **French**, **Germanic Languages**, **Slavic**, **Portuguese**, **Hebrew and Semitic Studies**, **Italian**, and **Asian Studies**. Another section, **Teaching With the Web**, gathers a host of sites offering teaching strategies and ideas. Language Links is neatly organized, and each link is accompanied by a brief description.

**HIGHLIGHTS FOR TEACHERS:** Within the blue box in the center of the home page, visitors will find a link to **Multi-Language Sites: Links for All Languages**. Visitors to this area will find newspapers, magazines, and radio stations in many languages. The area also contains City/Country Tours that give online visitors a taste of local culture around the world. Here, you can find the very cool **Language Trade** site, which connects two people from different countries who are interested in learning one another's language. Using the free Yahoo! Messenger tool, the two people may speak to each other at no cost.

One of the best resources in the **Teaching With the Web** section is **The Virtual Picture Album** site. These straightforward pictures allow teachers to introduce practical and focused vocabulary (particularly for such categories as animals, objects, natural phenomena, and cityscapes) and to depict situations where numerous events are occurring at the same time. The pictures also allow for the practice of particular grammatical constructions. Each picture is accompanied by a list of corresponding vocabulary items and suggested lesson topics and grammar points.

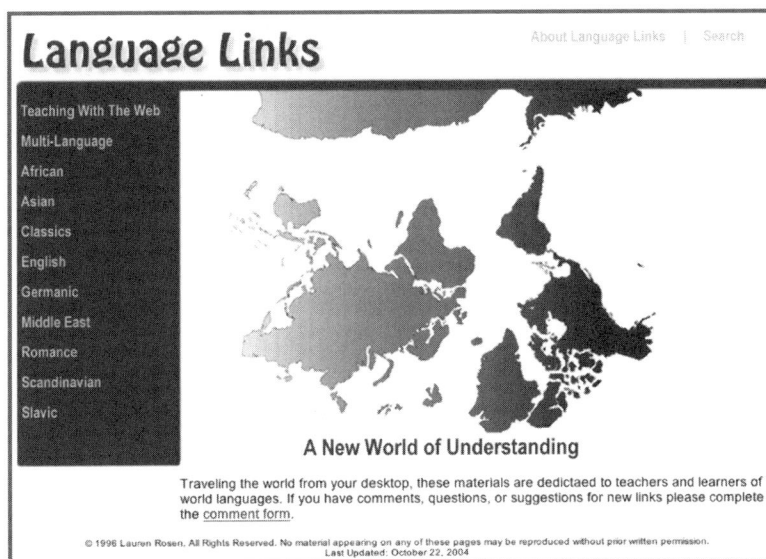

## Language Links

About Language Links | Search

Teaching With The Web
Multi-Language
African
Asian
Classics
English
Germanic
Middle East
Romance
Scandinavian
Slavic

**A New World of Understanding**

Traveling the world from your desktop, these materials are dedictaed to teachers and learners of world languages. If you have comments, questions, or suggestions for new links please complete the comment form.

© 1996 Lauren Rosen. All Rights Reserved. No material appearing on any of these pages may be reproduced without prior written permission.
Last Updated: October 22, 2004

## Marjorie Chan's China Links

### chinalinks.osu.edu

**SITE DESCRIPTION:** A number of other Web sites dealing with the study of Chinese language and culture deem Marjorie Chan's China Links to be the most comprehensive and essential resource on the Internet. Indeed, this site contains more than 600 links divided into four main areas: **ChinaLinks 1** (Search Engines, Chinese Studies, E-Texts, and Netnews); **ChinaLinks 2** (Chinese Language Software and AV Programs); **ChinaLinks 3** (Chinese Language and Linguistics); and **ChinaLinks 4** (General Linguistics and Internet Resources).

Each Web site is described briefly but tellingly, and Dr. Chan adds a considerable amount of useful information regarding the details of both Internet navigation and the complex process of representing Chinese characters on Western computers.

**HIGHLIGHTS FOR TEACHERS:** Teachers will probably find the Chinese Language and Linguistics area to be of greatest interest (listed on the home page as **ChinaLinks 3**). Within that area, the first section, Chinese Language Teaching and Learning Resources, is a good place to visit first.

Two resources here are of particular note: #19, **Learning Chinese Online**, by Tianwei Xie at California State University at Long Beach, and #33, **Teaching and Learning Chinese**, by Jianhua Bai at Kenyon College.

---

**Marjorie K.M. Chan**

ChinaLinks Home Page -- Table of Contents        ChinaLinks Search
ChinaLinks 1 - ChinaLinks 2 - ChinaLinks 3 - ChinaLinks 4                Advance

### ChinaLinks 3: Chinese Language and Linguistics

**H. CHINESE LANGUAGE TEACHING AND LEARNING RESOURCES:**

1. Study Abroad Chinese Language Schools. StudyAbroad.com's listings and links to institutions with study-abroad programs for Chinese (and other languages). See also Harvard U.'s links to Study Chinese Abroad Programs. (Or visit Escape Artist: Jobs in Asia for links to ESL and bilingual job opportunities.)
2. Archive of Chinese Teaching Materials: Advanced Level. Harvard U.'s downloadable, GB-encoded reading materials in MS Word format (for Windows).
3. C L A P. Chinese Learner's Alternate Page, from SinoLogic; updated weekly, this is a fun site for students learning Chinese.
4. CD's and Other Multimedia Programs for Learning Chinese. Tianwei Xie's **must-visit** webpage containing the Internet's most extensive set of links to online Chinese-learning software and vendors (e.g., Chinese Character Tutor - CyberChinese - Easy Chinese Learning CD ROM - HyperChina Interactive Chinese - Learn Chinese on CD-ROM - Professional Interactive Chinese - Power Chinese - Wenlin (version 3.0 includes an expanded version of John DeFrancis' *ABC Chinese-English Dictionary*, with over 10,000 characters and approximately 200,000 words and phrases), etc. Site also has online reviews of software programs by teachers who are currently using those programs; part of T. Xie's Learning Chinese Online (see below). For a stand-alone webpage of online reviews, see CLTA and Learning Chinese Online's Online Reviews: CALL Software for Chinese (NB: revised URL) Also see Clavis Sinica (for second-third year learners that includes a dictionary of 3750 characters in 12,000 entries), Besta's hand-held *Oxford Advanced Learner's English-Chinese Dictionary* below, and Commercial Press (HK) Ltd.'s *Hanyu Da Cidian CD-ROM* (part of my ChinaLinks2).
5. Centre of Research on Education in China (CREC). Website maintained at the University of Hong Kong, CREC was established in 1998 to provide support and coordination of research on China's education; to support visiting scholars who are doing research into China's education system; etc.

# SCREENSHOT CREDITS

## CHAPTER 1 • The Arts
Page 14: © The Minneapolis Institute of the Arts/The Walker Arts Center.
Page 15: By permission of the Center for Applied Research and Educational Improvement, College of Education and Human Development, University of Minnesota.
Page 16: © 2005, J. Paul Getty Trust.
Page 17: By permission of Florentine Films.
Page 18: © 2005 The Museum of Modern Art, MoMA.org.
Page 19: By permission of the National Gallery of Art.
Page 20: © 2005 Kern County Superintendent of Schools. Used with permission.

## CHAPTER 2 • College and Career Planning
Page 24: By permission of The Career Key: Choosing a Career.
Page 25: By permission of the College Board.
Page 26: By permission of FastWeb.
Page 27: © 2004 The New York Times Company. Reprinted with permission.
Page 28: By permission of O*NET OnLine.
Page 29: © Thomson Peterson's, a part of The Thomson Corporation and its licensors. All rights reserved.
Page 30: By permission of SparkNotes.
Page 31: © 2005 by Kathryn Hake. Used with permission.

## CHAPTER 3 • English
Page 36: By permission of American Literature on the Web.
Page 37: © 1993–2005 by Ted Nellen.
Page 38: By permission of English Language and Literature Resources.
Page 39: By permission of High School Journalism.
Page 40: By permission of John F. Barber, Ph.D.
Page 41: By permission of Media Literacy Clearinghouse.
Page 42: By permission of Meeting the Secondary Reading Challenge.
Page 43: By permission of The Moonlit Road.
Page 44: Courtesy of Online Poetry Classroom, a Web site of thhe Academy of American Poets. Used with permission.
Page 45: By permission of Purdue University Online Writing Lab.
Page 46: By permission of Ray Saitz.
Page 47: By permission of Teaching That Makes Sense.
Page 48: By permission of Carla Beard.
Page 49: By permission of The Write Site.
Page 50: © 2005 by W. W. Norton & Company, Inc. Used with permission.

## CHAPTER 4 • General Teacher Support
Page 54: © 2005 by The Annenberg Foundation. Reproduced with permission. Further reproduction is prohibited.
Page 55: AOL@SCHOOL is a registered trademark of America Online, Inc. The America Online, Inc. content, name, icons, and trademarks are used with permission.
Page 56: Blue Web'n: © 2004 SBC Knowledge Ventures, L.P. All rights reserved.
Page 57: © Education World, Inc.

Page 58: © 2005 Educational Web Adventures, L.L.P. (Eduweb®).
Page 59: By permission of the The Educator's Reference Desk.
Page 60: By permission of the eMINTS National Center.
Page 61: By permission of Glencoe/McGraw-Hill.
Page 62: By permission of MarcoPolo.
Page 63: By permission of the Public Broadcasting Service.
Page 64: By permission of The WebQuest Page.

## CHAPTER 5 • Health and PE
Page 68: © Tufts University Nutrition Navigator, produced by the Center on Nutrition Communication at the Friedman School of Nutrition Science and Policy.
Page 69: By permission of PE Central.
Page 70: By permission of PELINKS4U.
Page 71: By permission of Rice University, Center for Technology in Teaching and Learning.
Page 72: © 1995–2005 The Nemours Foundation.
Page 73: By permission of Wired for Health.

## CHAPTER 6 • Mathematics
Page 78: By permission of Curry Center for Technology and Teacher Education, the University of Virginia.
Page 79: By permission of Dr. Ron Eglash, Department of Science and Technology Studies, RPI.
Page 80: By permission of E-Examples.
Page 81: By permission of the Eisenhower National Clearinghouse.
Page 82: © 1999–2005 by the National Council of Teachers of Mathematics, Inc. All rights reserved. Used with permission.
Page 83: By permission of Cynthia Lanius.
Page 85: © 2005 Math Forum@Drexel. Used with permission of Drexel University.
Page 86: By permission of the Office of Mathematics, Science, and Technology Education, University of Illinois at Urbana-Champaign.
Page 87: By permission of the National Library of Virtual Manipulatives for Interactive Mathematics.
Page 88: By permission of Education Development Center, Inc.
Page 89: © 1994–2005 The Shodor Education Foundation.
Page 90: Tools for Understanding was developed from a grant from the U.S. Department of Education. Support was provided by the Microsoft Corporation.

## CHAPTER 7 • Science
Page 94: © ActionBioscience.org, an educational resource of the American Institute of Biological Sciences.
Page 95: By permission of Oregon Public Broadcasting and PBS, in association with PBS affiliates throughout the United States.
Page 96: By permission of Leif Saul.
Page 97: © 2005 American Chemical Society. Used with permission.
Page 98: © 2005 by F. James Holler and John P. Selegue, Department of Chemistry, University of Kentucky.
Page 99: By permission of ESTME Week.
Page 100: © Exploratorium. Used with permission.
Page 101: © 2005 Howard Hughes Medical Institute.
Page 103: © 2005 National Science Teachers Association. Reprinted with permission.

Page 104: By permission of the Physical Sciences Resource Center.

Page 105: By permission of G. Bothun, University of Oregon. Funded by the National Science Foundation.

Page 106: By permission of Jeff Whittaker.

Page 107: By permission of The Why Files.

## CHAPTER 8 • Social Studies

Page 112: By permission of the Center for History and New Media, George Mason University.

Page 113: © 2005 United Nations Cyberschoolbus, UN Department of Public Information's Outreach Division. Used with permission. All rights reserved.

Page 114: By permission of Steven Mintz and Sara McNeil.

Page 115: By permission of Doug Linder.

Page 116: By permission of History/Social Studies for K–12 Teachers.

Page 117: By permission of Humanities-Interactive.

Page 118: By permission of World History Online.

Page 119: By permission of iEARN.

Page 120: By permission of Internet History Sourcebooks Project.

Page 121: By permission of The Learning Page, The Library of Congress.

Page 123: © 2004, Newsweek, Inc. Used with permission.

Page 124: By permission of SCORE: History/Social Science, San Bernardino County Superintendent of Schools.

Page 125: © 2005 by Educators for Social Responsibility. Used with permission.

## CHAPTER 9 • Technology Integration

Page 130: By permission of Burien County Intermediate School District, Michigan Department of Education.

Page 131: © 1999–2002 Internet Innovations, Inc. All rights reserved.

Page 132: © 2005 The George Lucas Educational Foundation. All rights reserved. Printed with permission.

Page 133: By permission of the High Plains Regional Technology in Education Consortium.

Page 134: By permission of Susan Brooks and Bill Byles.

Page 135: By permission of the University of Northern Iowa, College of Education.

Page 136: By permission of Nicenet.

Page 137: © 2005 TechLEARNING. Used with permission.

## CHAPTER 10 • World Languages

Page 143: By permission of Joanna Porvin.

Page 144: By permission of iLoveLanguages.

Page 145: By permission of Lauren Rosen.

Page 146: By permission of Marjorie Chan.

# Correlation to NETS·S and NETS·T

Teachers who are engaged in coursework for credentialing or professional growth may be required to develop lesson plans based on educational technology. Every Web site listed in this book provides resources and materials that can help you implement the National Educational Technology Standards for Students (NETS·S) and Teachers (NETS·T).

The full text of these standards and performance indicators follows, along with a NETS correlation table for each chapter of the book. Next to every Web site name and URL is a matrix that indicates which of the NETS·S and NETS·T standards are related to the primary areas of emphasis contained on each site.

# NATIONAL EDUCATIONAL TECHNOLOGY STANDARDS FOR STUDENTS (NETS•S)

The National Educational Technology Standards for students are divided into six broad categories. Standards within each category are to be introduced, reinforced, and mastered by students. Teachers can use these standards as guidelines for planning technology-based activities in which students achieve success in learning, communication, and life skills.

1. **Basic operations and concepts**
   - Students demonstrate a sound understanding of the nature and operation of technology systems.
   - Students are proficient in the use of technology.

2. **Social, ethical, and human issues**
   - Students understand the ethical, cultural, and societal issues related to technology.
   - Students practice responsible use of technology systems, information, and software.
   - Students develop positive attitudes toward technology uses that support lifelong learning, collaboration, personal pursuits, and productivity.

3. **Technology productivity tools**
   - Students use technology tools to enhance learning, increase productivity, and promote creativity.
   - Students use productivity tools to collaborate in constructing technology-enhanced models, preparing publications, and producing other creative works.

4. **Technology communications tools**
   - Students use telecommunications to collaborate, publish, and interact with peers, experts, and other audiences.
   - Students use a variety of media and formats to communicate information and ideas effectively to multiple audiences.

5. **Technology research tools**
   - Students use technology to locate, evaluate, and collect information from a variety of sources.
   - Students use technology tools to process data and report results.
   - Students evaluate and select new information resources and technological innovations based on the appropriateness to specific tasks.

6. **Technology problem-solving and decision-making tools**
   - Students use technology resources for solving problems and making informed decisions.
   - Students employ technology in the development of strategies for solving problems in the real world.

# NATIONAL EDUCATIONAL TECHNOLOGY STANDARDS FOR TEACHERS (NETS•T)

**A**ll classroom teachers should be prepared to meet the following standards and performance indicators.

### I. Technology Operations and Concepts

Teachers demonstrate a sound understanding of technology operations and concepts. Teachers:

A. demonstrate introductory knowledge, skills, and understanding of concepts related to technology (as described in the ISTE National Educational Technology Standards for Students).

B. demonstrate continual growth in technology knowledge and skills to stay abreast of current and emerging technologies.

### II. Planning and Designing Learning Environments and Experiences

Teachers plan and design effective learning environments and experiences supported by technology. Teachers:

A. design developmentally appropriate learning opportunities that apply technology-enhanced instructional strategies to support the diverse needs of learners.

B. apply current research on teaching and learning with technology when planning learning environments and experiences.

C. identify and locate technology resources and evaluate them for accuracy and suitability.

D. plan for the management of technology resources within the context of learning activities.

E. plan strategies to manage student learning in a technology-enhanced environment.

### III. Teaching, Learning, and the Curriculum

Teachers implement curriculum plans that include methods and strategies for applying technology to maximize student learning. Teachers:

A. facilitate technology-enhanced experiences that address content standards and student technology standards.

B. use technology to support learner-centered strategies that address the diverse needs of students.

C. apply technology to develop students' higher-order skills and creativity.

D. manage student learning activities in a technology-enhanced environment.

## IV. Assessment and Evaluation

Teachers apply technology to facilitate a variety of effective assessment and evaluation strategies. Teachers:

A. apply technology in assessing student learning of subject matter using a variety of assessment techniques.

B. use technology resources to collect and analyze data, interpret results, and communicate findings to improve instructional practice and maximize student learning.

C. apply multiple methods of evaluation to determine students' appropriate use of technology resources for learning, communication, and productivity.

## V. Productivity and Professional Practice

Teachers use technology to enhance their productivity and professional practice. Teachers:

A. use technology resources to engage in ongoing professional development and lifelong learning.

B. continually evaluate and reflect on professional practice to make informed decisions regarding the use of technology in support of student learning.

C. apply technology to increase productivity.

D. use technology to communicate and collaborate with peers, parents, and the larger community in order to nurture student learning.

## VI. Social, Ethical, Legal, and Human Issues

Teachers understand the social, ethical, legal, and human issues surrounding the use of technology in PK–12 schools and apply that understanding in practice. Teachers:

A. model and teach legal and ethical practice related to technology use.

B. apply technology resources to enable and empower learners with diverse backgrounds, characteristics, and abilities.

C. identify and use technology resources that affirm diversity.

D. promote safe and healthy use of technology resources.

E. facilitate equitable access to technology resources for all students.

# NETS CORRELATION MATRIX

| The Arts | NETS FOR STUDENTS (NETS•S) | | | | | | NETS FOR TEACHERS (NETS•T) | | | | | |
|---|---|---|---|---|---|---|---|---|---|---|---|---|
| **Name of Site/URL** | 1 | 2 | 3 | 4 | 5 | 6 | I | II | III | IV | V | VI |
| **ArtsConnectEd**<br>www.artsconnected.org | | | | | | | | | | | | |
| **Arts for Academic Achievement:**<br>**The Annenberg Challenge**<br>education.umn.edu/CAREI/Reports/<br>Annenberg/ | | | | | | | | | | | | |
| **For Teachers (Getty Education)**<br>www.getty.edu/education/for_teachers | | | | | | | | | | | | |
| **Jazz**<br>www.pbs.org/jazz | | | | | | | | | | | | |
| **MoMA Educational Resources**<br>www.moma.org/education/<br>multimedia.html | | | | | | | | | | | | |
| **National Gallery of Art:**<br>**Education**<br>www.nga.gov/education/education.htm | | | | | | | | | | | | |
| **TeachingArts.org**<br>www.teachingarts.org | | | | | | | | | | | | |

The shaded boxes indicate standards related to the content of the Web site.

# NETS CORRELATION MATRIX

| College and Career Planning | NETS FOR STUDENTS (NETS•S) | | | | | | NETS FOR TEACHERS (NETS•T) | | | | | |
|---|---|---|---|---|---|---|---|---|---|---|---|---|
| Name of Site/URL | 1 | 2 | 3 | 4 | 5 | 6 | I | II | III | IV | V | VI |
| **The Career Key: Choosing a Career** www.careerkey.org | | | | | | | | | | | | |
| **College Board** www.collegeboard.com | | | | | | | | | | | | |
| **FastWeb** fastweb.monster.com | | | | | | | | | | | | |
| **The New York Times Learning Network** www.nytimes.com/learning/ | | | | | | | | | | | | |
| **O*NET Career Exploration Tools** www.onetcenter.org/tools.html | | | | | | | | | | | | |
| **Peterson's** www.petersons.com | | | | | | | | | | | | |
| **SparkNotes** sparknotes.com | | | | | | | | | | | | |
| **Vocational Information Center** www.khake.com | | | | | | | | | | | | |

The shaded boxes indicate standards related to the content of the Web site.

# NETS CORRELATION MATRIX

| English | NETS FOR STUDENTS (NETS•S) | | | | | | NETS FOR TEACHERS (NETS•T) | | | | | |
|---|---|---|---|---|---|---|---|---|---|---|---|---|
| **Name of Site/URL** | 1 | 2 | 3 | 4 | 5 | 6 | I | II | III | IV | V | VI |
| **American Literature on the Web** www.nagasaki-gaigo.ac.jp/ishikawa/amlit/ | | | | | | | | | | | | |
| **Cyber English** www.tnellen.com/cybereng/ | | | | | | | | | | | | |
| **English Language and Literature Resources** dewey.chs.chico.k12.ca.us/engl.html | | | | | | | | | | | | |
| **High School Journalism** highschooljournalism.org | | | | | | | | | | | | |
| **John F. Barber, Ph.D.** www.brautigan.net/john | | | | | | | | | | | | |
| **Media Literacy Clearinghouse** medialit.med.sc.edu | | | | | | | | | | | | |
| **Meeting the Secondary Reading Challenge** www.sarasota.k12.fl.us/sarasota/mainmenu.htm | | | | | | | | | | | | |
| **The Moonlit Road** www.themoonlitroad.com | | | | | | | | | | | | |
| **Online Poetry Classroom** www.onlinepoetryclassroom.org | | | | | | | | | | | | |
| **Online Writing Lab, Purdue University** owl.english.purdue.edu | | | | | | | | | | | | |
| **Outta Ray's Head: Lesson Plans, Handouts, and Ideas** home.cogeco.ca/~rayser3 | | | | | | | | | | | | |
| **Teaching That Makes Sense** www.ttms.org | | | | | | | | | | | | |
| **Web English Teacher** www.webenglishteacher.com | | | | | | | | | | | | |
| **The Write Site** www.writesite.org | | | | | | | | | | | | |
| **W. W. Norton & Company: Student Resources** www.wwnorton.com/college/titles/students/ | | | | | | | | | | | | |

The shaded boxes indicate standards related to the content of the Web site.

# NETS CORRELATION MATRIX

| General Teacher Support | NETS FOR STUDENTS (NETS•S) | | | | | | NETS FOR TEACHERS (NETS•T) | | | | | |
|---|---|---|---|---|---|---|---|---|---|---|---|---|
| Name of Site/URL | 1 | 2 | 3 | 4 | 5 | 6 | I | II | III | IV | V | VI |
| **Annenberg/CPB Learner.org** www.learner.org | | | | | | | | | | | | |
| **AOL@SCHOOL** www.aolatschool.com | | | | | | | | | | | | |
| **Blue Web'n** www.kn.sbc.com/wired/bluewebn | | | | | | | | | | | | |
| **Education World** www.educationworld.com | | | | | | | | | | | | |
| **Educational Web Adventures (Eduweb)** www.eduweb.com | | | | | | | | | | | | |
| **The Educator's Reference Desk** www.eduref.org | | | | | | | | | | | | |
| **eThemes** www.emints.org/ethemes/ | | | | | | | | | | | | |
| **Glencoe Online** www.glencoe.com/sec/ | | | | | | | | | | | | |
| **MarcoPolo** www.marcopolo-education.org | | | | | | | | | | | | |
| **PBS TeacherSource** www.pbs.org/teachersource/ | | | | | | | | | | | | |
| **The WebQuest Page** webquest.sdsu.edu | | | | | | | | | | | | |

The shaded boxes indicate standards related to the content of the Web site.

# NETS CORRELATION MATRIX

| Health and PE | NETS FOR STUDENTS (NETS•S) | | | | | | NETS FOR TEACHERS (NETS•T) | | | | | |
|---|---|---|---|---|---|---|---|---|---|---|---|---|
| **Name of Site/URL** | 1 | 2 | 3 | 4 | 5 | 6 | I | II | III | IV | V | VI |
| **Nutrition Navigator: A Rating Guide to Nutrition Web Sites** navigator.tufts.edu | | | | | | | | | | | | |
| **PE Central** www.pecentral.org | | | | | | | | | | | | |
| **PELINKS4U** www.pelinks4u.org | | | | | | | | | | | | |
| **The Reconstructors Solve Medical Mysteries** medmyst.rice.edu | | | | | | | | | | | | |
| **TeensHealth** www.kidshealth.org/teen/ | | | | | | | | | | | | |
| **Wired for Health** www.wiredforhealth.gov.uk | | | | | | | | | | | | |

The shaded boxes indicate standards related to the content of the Web site.

# NETS CORRELATION MATRIX

| Mathematics | NETS FOR STUDENTS (NETS•S) | | | | | | NETS FOR TEACHERS (NETS•T) | | | | | |
| --- | --- | --- | --- | --- | --- | --- | --- | --- | --- | --- | --- | --- |
| Name of Site/URL | 1 | 2 | 3 | 4 | 5 | 6 | I | II | III | IV | V | VI |
| Center for Technology and Teacher Education: Mathematics www.teacherlink.org/content/math/ | | | | | | | | | | | | |
| Culturally Situated Design Tools: Teaching Math Through Culture www.rpi.edu/~eglash/csdt.html | | | | | | | | | | | | |
| E-Examples standards.nctm.org/document/eexamples/ | | | | | | | | | | | | |
| Eisenhower National Clearing-house for Mathematics and Science Education (ENC) www.enc.org | | | | | | | | | | | | |
| Figure This! Math Challenges for Families www.figurethis.org | | | | | | | | | | | | |
| Fun Mathematics Lessons by Cynthia Lanius math.rice.edu/~lanius/Lessons/ | | | | | | | | | | | | |
| Learning Wave Communications: Engage Your Brain www.learningwave.com/menu.html | | | | | | | | | | | | |
| Math Forum@Drexel mathforum.org | | | | | | | | | | | | |
| Mathematics Materials for Tomorrow's Teachers www.mste.uiuc.edu/m2t2/ | | | | | | | | | | | | |
| National Library of Virtual Manipulatives for Interactive Mathematics matti.usu.edu/nlvm/nav/ | | | | | | | | | | | | |
| Problems with a Point www2.edc.org/mathproblems/ | | | | | | | | | | | | |
| Shodor Education Foundation www.shodor.org | | | | | | | | | | | | |
| Tools for Understanding www.ups.edu/community/tofu/ | | | | | | | | | | | | |

The shaded boxes indicate standards related to the content of the Web site.

# NETS CORRELATION MATRIX

| Science | NETS FOR STUDENTS (NETS•S) | | | | | | NETS FOR TEACHERS (NETS•T) | | | | | |
|---|---|---|---|---|---|---|---|---|---|---|---|---|
| Name of Site/URL | 1 | 2 | 3 | 4 | 5 | 6 | I | II | III | IV | V | VI |
| ActionBioscience.org<br>www.actionbioscience.org | X | X | X |  | X | X | X | X | X | X | X | X |
| American Field Guide<br>www.pbs.org/americanfieldguide/ | X | X | X |  | X | X | X | X | X | X | X | X |
| Biology in Motion<br>biologyinmotion.com | X | X | X |  | X | X | X | X | X |  | X | X |
| Chemistry.org<br>www.chemistry.org | X | X |  | X | X |  | X | X | X | X | X | X |
| The Comic Book Periodic Table of the Elements<br>www.uky.edu/Projects/Chemcomics/ | X | X |  | X | X | X | X | X |  |  | X | X |
| ESTME Web Site Gallery<br>www.estme.org/gallery/ | X | X | X | X | X | X | X | X | X | X | X | X |
| Exploratorium<br>www.exploratorium.edu | X | X | X | X | X | X | X | X | X | X | X | X |
| Howard Hughes Medical Institute's BioInteractive<br>www.biointeractive.org | X | X | X |  | X | X | X | X | X | X | X | X |
| NASA Education Enterprise<br>www.education.nasa.gov | X | X | X | X | X | X | X | X | X | X | X | X |
| National Science Teachers Association<br>www.nsta.org | X | X | X | X | X | X | X | X | X | X | X | X |
| Physical Sciences Resource Center<br>psrc.aapt.org |  | X | X | X | X | X | X | X | X |  | X | X |
| Physics Applets<br>jersey.uoregon.edu/vlab/ | X | X |  | X | X | X | X | X | X | X | X | X |
| PhysicsLessons.com<br>www.physicslessons.com | X | X | X | X | X | X | X | X | X | X | X | X |
| The Why Files<br>whyfiles.org | X | X | X | X | X | X | X | X | X |  | X | X |

The shaded boxes indicate standards related to the content of the Web site.

# NETS CORRELATION MATRIX

| Social Studies | NETS FOR STUDENTS (NETS•S) | | | | | | NETS FOR TEACHERS (NETS•T) | | | | | |
|---|---|---|---|---|---|---|---|---|---|---|---|---|
| Name of Site/URL | 1 | 2 | 3 | 4 | 5 | 6 | I | II | III | IV | V | VI |
| Center for History and New Media<br>chnm.gmu.edu | | | | | | | | | | | | |
| Cyberschoolbus: United Nations<br>www.cyberschoolbus.un.org | | | | | | | | | | | | |
| Digital History<br>www.digitalhistory.uh.edu | | | | | | | | | | | | |
| Famous Trials<br>www.law.umkc.edu/faculty/projects/<br>ftrials/ftrials.htm | | | | | | | | | | | | |
| History/Social Studies for K–12 Teachers<br>home.comcast.net/~dboals1/boals.html | | | | | | | | | | | | |
| Humanities-Interactive<br>www.humanities-interactive.org/<br>a_base_UD.html | | | | | | | | | | | | |
| HyperHistory Online<br>www.hyperhistory.com/online_n2/<br>History_n2/a.html | | | | | | | | | | | | |
| iEARN<br>www.iearn.org | | | | | | | | | | | | |
| Internet History Sourcebooks Project<br>www.fordham.edu/halsall/ | | | | | | | | | | | | |
| The Learning Page . . . Especially for Teachers<br>lcweb2.loc.gov/learn/ | | | | | | | | | | | | |
| National Geographic Education Guide<br>www.nationalgeographic.com/<br>education/ | | | | | | | | | | | | |
| Newsweek Education Program<br>www.newsweekeducation.com | | | | | | | | | | | | |
| SCORE: History/Social Science<br>score.rims.k12.ca.us | | | | | | | | | | | | |
| Special Projects: Understanding World Events<br>www.esrnational.org/sp/we/world.htm | | | | | | | | | | | | |

The shaded boxes indicate standards related to the content of the Web site.

# NETS CORRELATION MATRIX

| Technology Integration | NETS FOR STUDENTS (NETS•S) | | | | | | NETS FOR TEACHERS (NETS•T) | | | | | |
|---|---|---|---|---|---|---|---|---|---|---|---|---|
| Name of Site/URL | 1 | 2 | 3 | 4 | 5 | 6 | I | II | III | IV | V | VI |
| Best Practices of Technology Integration www.remc11.k12.mi.us/bstpract | | | | | | | | | | | | |
| Biopoint's Course Productivity WebTools www.biopoint.com/webtools/ coursetools.html | | | | | | | | | | | | |
| Edutopia (George Lucas Educational Foundation) www.glef.org | | | | | | | | | | | | |
| High Plains Regional Technology in Education Consortium www.hprtec.org | | | | | | | | | | | | |
| Internet4Classrooms www.internet4classrooms.com | | | | | | | | | | | | |
| InTime www.intime.uni.edu | | | | | | | | | | | | |
| Nicenet Internet Classroom Assistant www.nicenet.org | | | | | | | | | | | | |
| TechLEARNING.com: Technology & Learning www.techlearning.com | | | | | | | | | | | | |

The shaded boxes indicate standards related to the content of the Web site.

# NETS CORRELATION MATRIX

| World Languages | NETS FOR STUDENTS (NETS•S) | | | | | | NETS FOR TEACHERS (NETS•T) | | | | | |
|---|---|---|---|---|---|---|---|---|---|---|---|---|
| **Name of Site/URL** | 1 | 2 | 3 | 4 | 5 | 6 | I | II | III | IV | V | VI |
| **BBC Languages** <br> www.bbc.co.uk/languages | | | | | | | | | | | | |
| **Case de Joanna: Language Learning Resources** <br> www.casadejoanna.com | | | | | | | | | | | | |
| **iLoveLanguages** <br> www.ilovelanguages.com | | | | | | | | | | | | |
| **Language Links** <br> www.langlink.net | | | | | | | | | | | | |
| **Marjorie Chan's China Links** <br> chinalinks.osu.edu | | | | | | | | | | | | |

The shaded boxes indicate standards related to the content of the Web site.